SAMPSON TECHNICAL COLLEGE

YOUR CAREER IN

AIR CONDITIONING, REFRIGERATION & RELATED TECHNICAL OCCUPATIONS

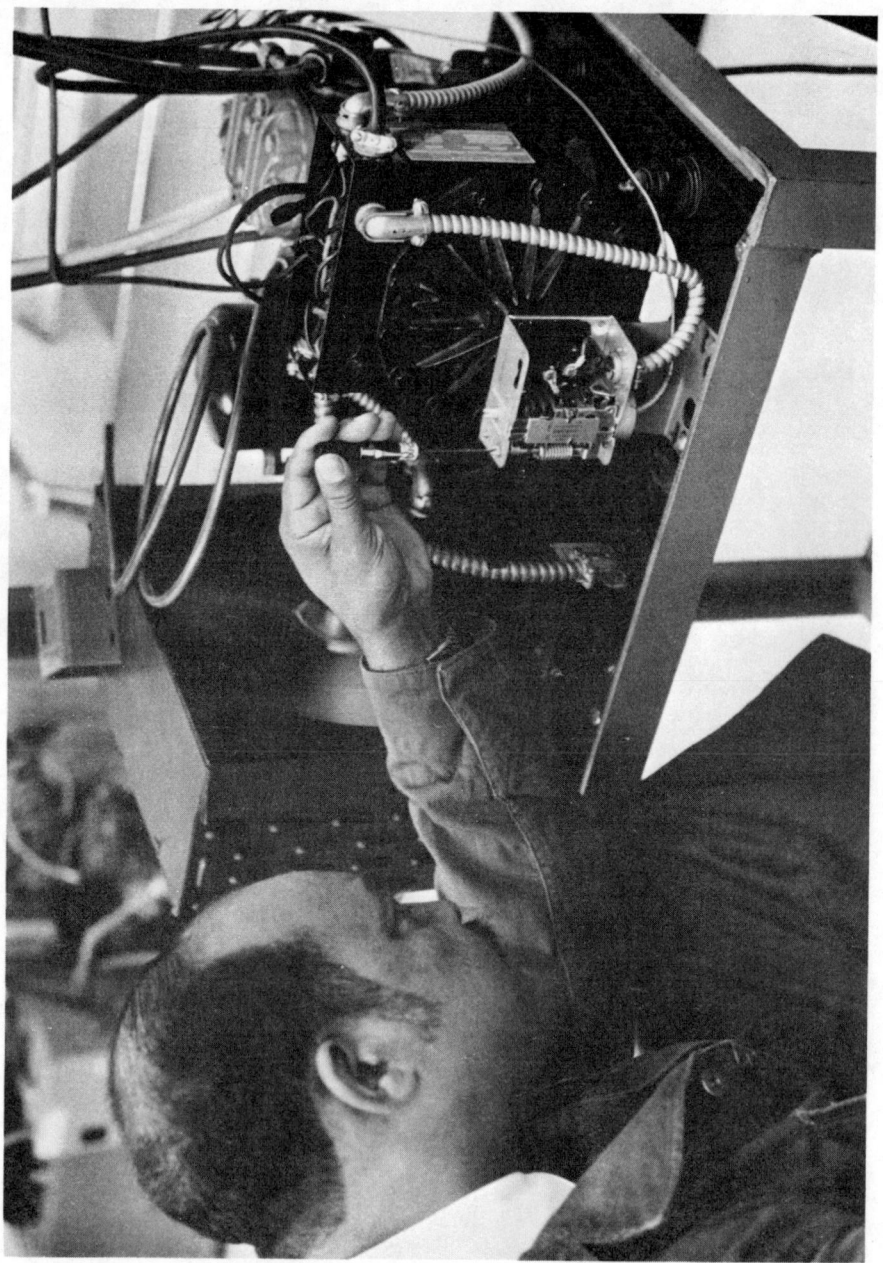

arco's
CAREER GUIDANCE SERIES

YOUR CAREER IN
AIR CONDITIONING, REFRIGERATION
AND RELATED
TECHNICAL OCCUPATIONS

Donald F. Daly

ARCO PUBLISHING, INC.
NEW YORK

Second Revised Edition

Part I of this Arco edition was originally published under the title *Your Future in Air Conditioning and Refrigeration*.

Published by Arco Publishing, Inc.
219 Park Avenue South, New York, N.Y. 10003

Copyright © 1968, 1971, 1979 by Donald F. Daly

All rights reserved. No part of this book may be reproduced in any form without written permission from the publisher, except by a reviewer.

Library of Congress Cataloging in Publication Data

Daly, Donald F
  Your career in air conditioning, refrigeration and related technical occupations.

  (Arco career guidance series)
  Published in 1971 under title: Your future in air conditioning and refrigeration.
  1. Refrigeration and refrigerating machinery—Vocational guidance.   2. Air conditioning—Vocational guidance.
  I. Title.
  TP492.7.D27   1978   621.5'6'023   78-701

ISBN 0-668-04562-0 (Library Edition)
ISBN 0-668-04573-6 (Paper Edition)

Printed in the United States of America

Contents

	About This Book	7
	Foreword	9

PART I

I.	Early History	17
II.	How to Get a Job	21
III.	Basic Educational Requirements	30
IV.	The Best Job for You	43
V.	Cold Storage and Institutional Refrigeration	53
VI.	Marine Refrigeration	59
VII.	Automative Air Conditioning and Transport Refrigeration	65
VIII.	Sales Jobs	74
IX.	Your Own Business as a Contractor-Serviceman	80
X.	Residential Air Conditioning Contract Service	87
XI.	Maintenance and Operations Foreman	96
XII.	Financing Your Technical Education	106
XIII.	Vocational/Technical Education Is Big Business	112
XIV.	Directory	119
XV.	Biographical Sketches	128

PART II

I.	Changing Fashions in Vocational/Technical Education	143
II.	Investigate Before You Invest	152
III.	Make the Most of Your Vocational Training Program	161
IV.	Work Habits, Job Attitudes and Career Hangups	169

About This Book

Every student or trainee who expects to prepare for a rewarding career in any branch of the air conditioning and refrigeration industry should be prepared to assume much of the responsibility for his own educational destiny. This will not be easy, but it would help if every student could have an opportunity to sit down for a long conversation with twenty of the most knowledgeable industry employers, shop and field supervisors, leading technicians, trade school instructors and vocational guidance experts.

If this could be done, in all probability, one of two things would follow. Either the student would abandon his plans for a career in this industry, or his chances for success would be greatly enhanced.

Public and private trade/technical schools, industry sponsored training programs, home-study schools and labor/management sponsored apprentice training programs have always provided a means for ambitious individuals to prepare for good jobs in air conditioning, heating, refrigeration technology, building and construction technology, maintenance and service technology, and related engineering occupations. The technical education made possible by such training, when combined with on-the-job experience, can produce the highly skilled technicians and service mechanics who are so much in demand.

It would, however, be a serious mistake to believe that just any course of air conditioning and refrigeration technology, followed by a random amount of on-the-job experience, will produce the highly qualified individuals that industry employers are so anxious to hire. Fortunately, career preparation for these occupations is just not all that easy.

For best results every student and trainee should have his own, well organized, do-it-yourself career development program. In this regard, however, one very important fact should be noted—the *quality* of vocational/technical education is of far greater importance than the *quantity*, and that is what this book is all about. Information has been drawn from many sources.

Any attempt to list all of the concerned individuals who made a contribution to this book would result in an acknowledgement section that would be longer than the book itself. This is true because the research involved covered quite a long period of time and included interviews, and an exchange of ideas, with several hundred industry employers, shop and field supervisors, technicians, instructors, students, trainees and others who are in the mainstream of every branch of the industry.

My own background for writing in this field dates back many years to the time when my first job information article was published in one of the leading air conditioning and refrigeration industry trade journals. Since that date I have worked in, and continued my close association with, many branches of the industry. I am also deeply indebted to the editors of industry trade publications who have used my articles over the years.

This is important to this book because the research for these writing projects produced far more material than could be used in a feature article. It would not be feasible to list all of these publications, but they include *Air Conditioning, Heating and Refrigeration News*; *Contractor Magazine*; *Consumer Bulletin*; *Overdrive*; *Western Trucking*; *Wheels Afield*; *Appliance Service News*; *Refrigeration Service and Contracting*, and others.

To these sources must be added the research that went into the writing of four vocational guidance books. All of these articles and books were intended to provide information and guide-lines that would help students, trainees and technicians to evaluate career and business opportunities in many branches of the huge, but fragmented, air conditioning, heating and refrigeration industry.

The information contained in this book should make it possible for the career-wise individual, who aspires to master any of these occupational fields, to make the most of his vocational/technical education and related on-the-job experience. (The ball is in your court. Or, if you prefer, "The monkey is on your back.")

Foreword

The refrigeration and air-conditioning industry has been expanding since the day it was established, and industry leaders are unanimous in their conviction that this growth will continue. One thing, however, could slow this growth—the increasing shortage of skilled technicians who will be needed to sell, install, service, and maintain the millions of new refrigeration and air-conditioning units that will be put into service over the next ten years.

The shortage of technically qualified men will be felt in every branch of the industry, but it will be most apparent in the newer fields, where the growth rate is highest. These new applications of refrigeration and air conditioning will open up a new class of job, requiring a level of technical training and experience not achieved by many of the mechanics now working in this field. Skilled men will be much in demand, and job opportunities will cover the full range of technicians, mechanics, operating engineers, plant engineers, and mechanical plant superintendents. The following outlines give a brief description of some of the newer fields.

Residential Air Conditioning

In early 1977 less than 40 percent of all homes and apartments in the United States had air conditioning, but these figures do not tell the entire story. In the past a home or apartment was considered air-conditioned if any type of mechanical air-conditioning equipment was installed. By modern standards a very large number of these older systems would be classed as inadequate.

Engineers and home builders have now developed what they term a *total-comfort* concept for residential heating, ventilation, and air-conditioning. This new concept involves such elements as design, insulation, noise control, air distribution, humidity control, and air cleaning, in addition to heating and cooling. When properly designed and engineered to the needs of a specific residence, the total-comfort system for heating and cooling will be no more costly to install, no more costly to operate, and much more effective than the older systems.

As homeowners and apartment dwellers become more knowledgeable on the subject of home heating and air conditioning, they will demand this new type of installation, but this branch of the industry will not reach its full potential until it develops many technicians who are qualified to install, service, and maintain these more complex systems. The field will offer many fine job opportunities for qualified men, as well as opportunities for the establishment of an independent service shop.

Clean Rooms

The *clean-room* concept of air conditioning is used in laboratory research, precision assembly, hospital operating rooms, and many aerospace projects. This concept involves total control of all environmental conditions within a given space—usually a limited space. The clean room used in industry and the total-comfort idea for home air conditioning have much in common, but the high cost of such installations has limited their use.

If air-pollution problems continue to grow, however, it is possible that the clean room–total comfort concept will be modified and used in apartment houses, hotels, office buildings, industrial plants and, in time, whole communities. This branch of refrigeration and air conditioning will offer a growing number of good jobs for qualified men and many chances to start an independent service business in a field that is not overcrowded.

Office Buildings, Convention Facilities, Sports Arenas

One of the fastest-growing branches of the refrigeration and air-conditioning industry is the sector that includes exposition centers, office buildings, civic centers, sports arenas, and all types of commercial and industrial installations. The modern trend to high-rise buildings or groups of buildings in a single complex has brought the development of large central mechanical plants to provide hot water, heating, air conditioning, ventilation, refrigeration, and other services—and with it a need for many more skilled installers, service technicians, operating engineers, and plant engineers.

Jobs in this field run from that of semiskilled maintenance man to operating engineer, service technician, and building superintendent. This may well be the largest single field of opportunity in the industry. Such jobs offer a challenge, the pay is good, the working conditions are among the best, and the chances for advancement are virtually unlimited. In this field there are far more employers looking for qualified men than there are men looking for jobs. Since many property owners prefer to contract out service and maintenance work, this would be a fine field for an independent service business.

Food Stores and Supermarkets

In 1977 more than 1,500 new supermarkets were built and 1,250 older stores were remodeled and enlarged. This is one of the older branches of the refrigeration industry and growth will be in line with population changes. Since 1970 thousands of mini-supermarkets, such as Circle-K, Jiffy-Food-Stores and Mini-Marts, have been built. This will change the supermarket pattern to some degree.

The men who seek jobs in this field should understand that the experience and technology requirements are more closely related to refrigeration than to air conditioning. This means that the mechanic or technician deals with more complex equipment and the refrigerated storage spaces cover a much wider range of temperature control. Jobs are to be found in independent service contracting shops, factory branch shops, and shops operated by store chains. The field offers many opportunities for the establishment of an independent service shop.

Automotive and Truck-Cab Air Conditioning

Automotive air conditioning has had a phenomenal growth in recent years and this growth will continue. By mid-1977 more than 30,000,000 units were in service. The energy crisis has changed the product mix, since small imports and compact cars will soon make up to 50 percent of the new car market.

About 80 percent of all auto air-conditioning units are installed at the factory. Because it is not feasible for a car owner to take his car to the factory when the air-conditioning unit needs service, such work is done in local shops. This means many fine jobs for technicians who have the flexibility to take advantage of the opportunities that will develop as the field expands, and many chances to establish an independent sales, installation, and service agency.

Sales

Every man who works as a refrigeration and air-conditioning mechanic or technician should give some thought to the idea of selling on a full-time basis. Nearly all of the men who work for dealer-contractors are encouraged to push the sale of spare parts, supplies, and replacement equipment, and most employers are happy to pay for this extra effort. The idea of becoming a salesman or sales engineer is not at all farfetched.

The salesman who knows his product—its function, operation, and application—is far better equipped to sell it than the man who lacks such knowledge. This accounts for the fact that many present-day salesmen and sales engineers in the refrigeration and air-conditioning field have come up from the ranks of installation and service technicians.

Refrigeration Service Is Not a Do-It-Yourself Project

The fact that refrigeration and air-conditioning installation, maintenance, and service are not adapted to a do-it-yourself type of operation gives the mechanics of this trade, and the independent service contractor, a measure of protection that is not enjoyed by many mechanical trades and repair shops. The average homeowner may try to overhaul the engine of his car, remodel his home, or build a patio, but he seldom tries to repair or service the refrigeration, air-conditioning, or heating equipment in his home. And when he does, there is a strong possibility that his attempt will end in failure if not near-disaster. To do this work successfully, a mechanic must have special knowledge, special tools, and several items of special equipment. Refrigeration and air-conditioning installation and service is one field that will not be undercut by moonlighters.

An Independent Service Business

A recent survey of the refrigeration and air-conditioning sales, installation, and service industry revealed that up to 90 percent of all independent shops were owned and operated by men who had served an apprenticeship in the trade. Many of these shops, including the largest, started as a one-man operation in which the owner sold his knowledge and experience directly to the customer in the form of maintenance and service labor.

This is a proven method for establishing an independent service shop, and it works just as well in 1978 as it did in 1918. From the very first day of operation the independent service contractor can supplement his income by the sale of parts, supplies, refrigerants, and replacement equipment. Over a period of time such sales can overshadow the income from the sale of service labor.

About the Author

DONALD F. DALY has been in the mainstream of refrigeration and air-conditioning construction, service, and operations for many years, in close association with the technicians, mechanics, supervisors, contractors, and engineers in the field.

Born in Hamilton, Montana, Daly moved to California at an early age. After graduation from high school, he served in the U.S. Navy, the Merchant Marine, and the U.S. Coast Guard. He then attended a technical college for the study of refrigeration and air-conditioning technology.

After operating his own contracting business for a number of years, he joined a large contracting engineering company as an applications and test engineer. This work included supervision, inspection, and testing of large installations for ships, industrial plants, and defense projects. He worked in this capacity at the Atomic Energy Commission installation at Hanford, Washington; the Reactor Test Station at Arco, Idaho; and at Edwards and Vandenberg Air Force and Missile Bases in California.

He is the author of books and numerous articles in his field as well as articles on technical subjects for such magazines as *Consumer Bulletin, Motor West, Southern Motor Cargo,* and *Overdrive.* He recently retired from active field work, but he continues to write for industry publications.

DE WY'S Photo

CHAPTER I

Early History

In the early days of mechanical refrigeration, before small machines were developed for use in homes, food stores, and other commercial establishments, the cooling equipment used in ice and cold-storage plants was massive in size and operated under high pressure. Much of this machinery was steam powered, and the responsibility for its operation and maintenance was in the hands of licensed operating engineers, master mechanics, and a plant superintendent.

When manufacturers started to produce refrigerating machines small enough to be installed in homes, stores, and bars and for other commercial uses, a whole new field of opportunity was opened to ambitious men who had some mechanical aptitude. Starting in about 1918, and over the next twenty-five years, millions of small to medium-sized mechanical refrigeration units were produced and put into service.

The development of these low-pressure refrigeration machines and their expanding use received wide publicity, and many men were attracted to the field. Since this was a new field, it was necessary to train mechanics and technicians in the skills needed to demonstrate, sell, install, and service the equipment. For many years the burden of training fell on the manufacturers and distributors, but as the need for trained men became known, public and private schools were established and training texts became available.

For the first few years these small refrigeration machines were simple in design and covered a rather narrow range of temperature control within a cabinet or storage room. The degree of training and skill needed to install and service these units was not great, and any man who had a little mechanical aptitude could quickly become proficient at the work. Further simplifying the training needs, the publicity given this new field attracted many men who were already qualified in another mechanical trade.

Over the years, however, and as the market for these simple machines became saturated, engineers and manufacturers designed and produced refrigeration equipment that had a much broader range of cooling capability. The development of more complex machinery brought a need for many more mechanics and technicians, and these individuals had to develop a much higher degree of skill than had formerly been needed.

Until recently the public and private schools and the industry-sponsored training facilities were able to turn out enough skilled men to supply the demand.

Within the last two or three years, however, it became obvious that this was no longer true, and educators and vocational experts took steps to train more men. Unfortunately, early moves to correct the shortage of skilled manpower were geared to produce only limited-skill specialists, rather than the highly skilled technicians and mechanics who were needed.

Factors that have aggravated the training problem have been the development of entirely new specialties within the refrigeration and air-conditioning industry and the rapid expansion of some of the older branches. The new and fast-growing applications include automotive air conditioning, truck-cab air conditioning, transport refrigeration, containers, etc. Among the older branches of the industry that have shown great growth over the past few years are residential air conditioning and all types of refrigeration and air-conditioning equipment used in schools, hospitals, public buildings, and industrial plants.

The one thing that has complicated the training problem above all others is the fact that the new and specialized areas of the industry have not assumed the responsibility for training mechanics and technicians to demonstrate, sell, install, and service the equipment they produce. In many instances the men needed for this new work have been pirated from the older branches; such pirating of skilled manpower is not new, but it has caused much bitterness within the trade. The problem may grow worse before it is solved, but it is a plus factor for men who seek a career in this field. This is assuming, of course, that such men have the needed technical education, training, and experience; employers do not try to pirate limited-skill technicians.

Since the earliest days of small refrigeration machines, ambitious men have been drawn to this field because they saw in it an opportunity to own their own business. For the first years of this expanding field, such men hoped to own an appliance store and to sell, install, and service domestic and commercial refrigeration units and other home appliances. This ambition is still valid; however, men now have broader possibilities in the field.

In fact, an appliance store may not offer the best chance to establish a business. With so much refrigeration, air-conditioning, and heating equipment now in use, and more being sold every day, the best chance for success in an independent business might be in the service and maintenance field. In this type of business a qualified technician or mechanic can sell his experience, knowledge, and skill direct to the customer in the form of service labor, and add to his income by the sale of parts, supplies, refrigerants, and replacement equipment. Many mechanics have taken this route to the establishment of an independent business, and a surprising number of them have succeeded.

There is a need for a greatly expanded system of service shops for refrigeration and air-conditioning equipment. In fact, there is much evidence to prove that retail customers are becoming dissatisfied with both the quantity and the quality of the mechanical service that is available. This dissatisfaction, if permitted to grow, could have grave consequences for every segment of the industry.

The manufacturers of home-refrigerators, freezers, and package-type air-conditioning units have always given a good guarantee on such merchandise and have stood behind that guarantee.

Unfortunately, much of the new equipment being installed does not lend itself to the same class of service that has been used for home appliances. Technicians in this field must have more training and more experience.

It is possible that equipment manufacturers will solve many of their service problems by means of franchised service shops; but there will always be a place for the independent service contractor, and his success will hinge on one thing—his personal relationship with his service customers. No manufacturer's service organization can offer this personal relationship. The road to success is as simple as that.

CHAPTER II

How to Get a Job

The men who look for jobs in refrigeration and air conditioning as apprentices, helpers, technicians, mechanics, and operating engineers fall into two distinct groups. The first group includes those who have completed a sizable percentage of their technical education and who have had enough on-the-job experience to qualify as junior mechanic, technician, or operating engineer. The second group includes those who aspire to a career in the refrigeration and air-conditioning service industry, but who have just started their technical education and have had limited work experience.

The employment opportunities of these two groups are quite different, and this should be clearly understood. The men who have completed a meaningful amount of technical training and have had a few years of field experience will find many jobs open to them. Even more important, these men will have a better understanding of the job opportunities in the field and will know where the best jobs are to be found.

On the other hand, the men who are just starting their technical training and have had limited work experience may find that jobs that will help them to master one of the trades in this industry are not easy to obtain. The old story about having to have experience in order to get a job, but not being able to get the experience without a job, is more than a gag—it is a grim reality. However, it is a reality that has been mastered many times in the past, and it might be called the first real test of a man's determination to succeed in the career of his choice. Most of the information presented in this chapter is for the guidance of men who are just starting in this business.

It is a fact that most employers try to hire men who are fully qualified by training and experience for the work they are to do, but not all employers follow this policy. In the many specialty branches of the refrigeration and air-conditioning sales, installation, and service business, each job calls for a different degree of skill and technical education. In some instances, extensive experience in a special field can be a handicap to technicians, who find it impossible to unlearn the work habits and procedures acquired in other jobs.

For this reason many employers are willing to hire a man who has had limited experience, especially if that man has proven his intent to qualify for a better job by means of a course of formal study. Under these conditions an employer can train the man in his own methods, and the employee can direct his educational activities to suit the needs of his job.

Another important element in employment is the fact that many jobs in the refrigeration and air-conditioning industry do not require extensive training or work experience. The pay rates are in keeping with the training requirements; however, many of these secondary jobs do allow a student-worker to gain valuable experience, and they should be a part of every formal, or informal, apprenticeship.

The question of pay rates for student-workers is important; and it would be wise for the student to adjust his expectations to the realities of the situation. This does not mean that a student should allow an employer to take advantage of him by accepting very low wages in order to gain experience. However, he should not lose sight of one important fact: All jobs held during the training period should have but one purpose—to provide on-the-job experience that will enable the student to make practical use of the technical knowledge he is acquiring in his school work.

A few months of work in a busy shop, where a learner is allowed to work with mechanics and technicians on the actual installation, service, and operation of equipment, could have more career value than two or three years of work in a shop where all jobs were routine and offered little chance for the student to gain a variety of experience or to exercise his own initiative.

In many instances the beginning student in refrigeration and air conditioning will be able to offer an employer little more than a "warm body," a willingness to work, and an eagerness to learn. Fortunately, there is a place in many shops for men in this category. However, if the student hopes to progress in his career, he must take immediate steps to escape from this classification. Good attitudes are important to a beginning employee; the ability to get along with fellow employees, to take an interest in the business, to show initiative, and to assume a measure of responsibility are qualities that are highly prized by all employers and supervisors.

It would not be wise to quote wage rates a student-worker might expect to receive, but the wage patterns used in a formal apprenticeship can be used as a guide. The apprentice, in most instances, is paid a starting wage that is 50 percent of the journeyman rate. He will receive, if his school and work record are satisfactory, regular raises at six-month intervals until he graduates to journeyman. Thus, if the wage scale for journeymen was $8.00 per hour, the apprentice or helper would start at $4.00 per hour. (The wage rates quoted here are for illustrative purposes only and should not be applied to any specific job or employer. In addition, no mention has been made of fringe benefits that can add as much as 10 percent to base pay.)

When a person plans a course of training and work experience that will take several years to complete and that will lead to a lifetime career, decisions should be made with care. If the choice is refrigeration and air conditioning, it would be wise to select the specialty within the industry that will offer the best opportunity and the best hope for successful completion. However, the education and training program should not be too rigid, and it should be within the limits of what is reasonable and possible. The student should also give some thought to the job and business opportunities that will be open to him in the area where he hopes to make his home.

In other chapters of this book the education, training, and experience requirements for many jobs in refrigeration and air-conditioning sales, installation, service, and operation will be outlined. The student-worker should look for jobs in any, or all, of these fields. The following job-hunting methods have been used with some degree of success. However, many jobs in the refrigeration and air-conditioning service field will be found in shops that employ only a few men. Such jobs are obtained by direct application to the employer. Appearance and attitudes are of the utmost importance, but in the case of a student-worker the most compelling element in any job application might be the fact that you are trying to build a future in the business. The best recommendation you could offer would be evidence of progress in a technical training program. In addition, use all of the following job-hunting methods:

1. *School Employment Agencies.*
2. *State Employment Agencies.*
3. *Private Employment Agencies.*
4. *Veterans and Armed Service Employment Agencies.*
5. *City, County, State, and Federal Civil Service Commissions.*
6. *Every Employer in the Area That Is Known to Hire for This Field.*
7. *Social and Business Contacts.* The student should scrutinize his list of friends, acquaintances, business associates, and relatives to determine if any are in a position to offer employment, give advice on the subject, or give a character or work recommendation that might carry some weight.
8. *Civil Service Jobs.* Most city, county, state, and federal civil service commissions hire apprentices, helpers, technicians, and mechanics in the refrigeration and air-conditioning trades, or for closely related jobs such as maintenance men, operating assistants, etc. In addition, many of these commissions have an

employment policy that includes part-time work for students, especially for the vacation months when extra help is needed. The fact that an applicant is enrolled in a trade-technical training program and can show that he is making progress will enhance the prospects for employment.

9. *Local Refrigeration and Air-Conditioning Service Shops.* If jobs of the type sought are scarce, the student-worker should canvass every refrigeration and air-conditioning sales, installation, and service shop in his district. This effort should be extended to every business and industry that is known to employ mechanics, helpers, or operators for this field, including ice and cold-storage plants, meat-packing plants, food-processing plants, transport refrigeration shops, auto and truck-cab air-conditioning shops, etc. Here again, enrollment in a trade-technical training program could help to land a job.

10. *Refrigeration and Air-Conditioning Supply Stores.* Supply stores that deal exclusively in refrigeration and air-conditioning parts and components play an important part in the exchange of information that could lead to a job. The owners, managers, countermen, and clerks are in constant communication with the key men in every phase of the local industry. They know the employers who might want to hire a helper or mechanic, they know who might like to change jobs, and they know the qualified men who are looking for a job.

In addition, and perhaps even more important, the local refrigeration and air-conditioning supply store is a meeting place for all the men who work in the industry. Its staff members dispense a constant flow of technical information, and they often act as agents for manufacturers and distributors in industrywide educational and training programs. They have the latest industry news, and they are up on the industry gossip that is currently making the rounds. The student-worker should visit these stores to take part in the educational and social activities that originate in them and to seek the friendship and help of the employees. This can be a mutually beneficial arrangement in that it does their business no harm to bring an employer and an employee together. It should be noted, however, that this is seldom done from a profit motive alone; the most popular supply stores take on some of the character of a social and business club.

11. *The Refrigeration Service Engineers Society.* Founded in 1934, the Society now has more than 20,000 members and 300 local chapters. It is a nonprofit educational organization, and its members hold key jobs in every branch of the refrigeration and air-conditioning sales, installation, service, and operation field. The constitution of the Society forbids any noneducational activities, but it works very closely with many public and private trade-technical schools.

Every man who expects to make a career in this field would be wise to investigate what the Society has to offer. If there is a local chapter, application for membership may be made through the local Secretary. If there is no local chapter the individual might be eligible for a membership-at-large, which gives full benefits. Provision is also made for student members and associate members. The National Society also publishes a monthly magazine that goes to all members. For information, write to Refrigeration Service Engineers Society, 2720 Des Plaines Avenue, Des Plaines, Illinois 60018.

12. *Résumés, Interviews, and Applications.* Job application forms play an important part in any job hunt, especially when the applicant is dealing with employers who hire through a personnel department. There is no way to avoid the filling out of such forms, so the best approach is to make it a minor project to become proficient in this activity.

Probably the easiest way to become proficient in the filling out of application forms is to obtain sample forms from local hiring agencies and practice on them. One good source is the Post Office, where application forms for federal employment can be had for the asking. Other good sources are city, county, and state civil service commissions and the personnel department of any business or industry.

Job application forms must be filled out completely, and every question must be answered. If possible a typewriter should be used, but printing or handwriting are acceptable. In any case, the information given should be expressed clearly and be easy to read. When a personnel clerk comes across an application that is hard to read and understand, he will not spend a lot of time trying to ferret out the intended meaning. It is much easier just to put it aside and reach for one that is clear. When the job seeker has filled out a variety of forms and has mastered the process to the extent that he has produced a sample that is neat and free of mistakes, it would be a good idea to have copies made for future reference.

Job résumés and interviews comprise a broad and very important subject, which is too complex to be covered in a page or two. The serious job seeker should give much thought to his attitude during an interview. It is best not to be too aggressive. Allow the interviewer to take the lead and ask the questions. Do not get off the immediate question, and do not volunteer too much information. If you have submitted a résumé the interviewer has most of the information he needs, and his aim now is to determine whether the résumé is accurate or exaggerated and to form an opinion of your personality.

The formal résumé has become a large factor in job hunting, and its importance cannot be overstressed. If the résumé is poorly constructed, the applicant may never get as far as the interview. Many men seek professional aid in preparing a résumé, but it is wise to make sure that the expert really is a "pro." Many practitioners in this field are self-styled experts, with no real training or aptitude for the work.

The job seeker who has completed a large part of his trade-technical education and has had a few years of field experience will have a much broader occupational field to survey. At this point he will begin to reap the benefits of the time he has invested in training. The graduate student will be made aware of the many fine jobs that are open to a well-qualified technician, mechanic, or operating engineer. If he has not yet found a job that allows him to use his education to the fullest potential, he can look for a more suitable job by all the methods outlined here. However, the man in this position is not limited to these channels.

One of the best sources of job information is the classified ad sections of the industry trade journals and publications. If the applicant wants to offer his services he may place an ad in one or more of such publications. When he receives replies, he can then follow directions concerning application forms, résumés, and interviews.

If the applicant wants to answer ads in the classified section, he sends a letter and his job résumé to as many employers as he wishes; it is not necessary to mail to only one employer at a time. The job résumé can be photocopied, but a separate covering letter should be composed for each employer.

A list of trade journals and trade publications for the refrigeration and air-conditioning industry will be found at the back of this book. Nearly all of these magazines publish help-wanted ads; however, most of them are somewhat specialized and cover a limited branch of the industry. The one publication that covers several branches and also carries a large number of help-wanted ads is *Air Conditioning, Heating & Refrigeration News*. The editors of this weekly, newspaper-style publication range far and wide in their search for industry news, technical information, and business articles.

The *News*, because it is a weekly, publishes the greatest number and variety of help-wanted ads of all the industry publications. The subscription cost is $21.00 per year, which includes the annual Directory. Address: *Air Conditioning, Heating & Refrigeration News*, P.O. Box 6000, Birmingham, Michigan 48012.

When the time comes for the job seeker to examine the help-wanted ads in the *News* and other industry publications, he will make a startling discovery—THERE ARE FAR MORE JOBS SEEKING MEN THAN THERE ARE MEN SEEKING JOBS!

CHAPTER III

Basic Educational Requirements

The person who first said, "You can't get there from here," probably meant to be facetious, but when an attempt is made to evaluate the educational requirements that would qualify a man for a good job in refrigeration and air conditioning the remark takes on a rather grim reality. It might be rather difficult to "get there" from any conventional program that is available to the average man seeking a career in this field.

Jobs in refrigeration and air-conditioning sales, installation, maintenance, service, and operation cut across every segment of commerce, industry, and home ownership. They range from that of the semiskilled handyman who performs the simplest operational and maintenance tasks, to the plant superintendent who is responsible for the operation and maintenance of mechanical systems that may have cost several million dollars, to say nothing of the safety and comfort of hundreds of men and women who occupy the buildings under his care.

Another obstacle that lies in the path of the man who hopes to acquire the needed basic and technical education to qualify for a good job in refrigeration and air conditioning is the fact that this is an industry with many specialized branches. In fact, the field is so broad that no one man could encompass it in its entirety. For this reason, the ambitious man who seeks a career in this field should acquire a basic education that will form a solid foundation for the technical education needed to qualify for a good job.

A comprehensive investigation of the job and independent-business opportunities that are available in the industry—which included interviews with many dealer-contractors, supervisors,

PHOTO BY CARRIER AIR CONDITIONING TRAINING CENTER

Teaching aids of this type are widely used in trade-technical schools and industry-sponsored training programs. This Carrier Refrigeration Cycle Trainer displays all components that make up a conventional air-conditioning system. Windows in evaporator coil allow students to observe refrigerant behavior throughout the refrigeration cycle. Service problems can be simulated for diagnosis by students.

employers, trade-school instructors, personnel managers, and others active in the field—revealed many conflicting views on the subject of basic and technical education requirements. However, most of those interviewed agreed that it would be wise for a man to start preparing for such a career while still in high school. From that point, if at all possible, he should continue his education through a college-level course in Refrigeration and Air-Conditioning Technology that would earn him an Associate in Science degree. This level of training is available in many public and private trade-technical colleges.

The following outlines of basic educational requirements are intended as a basis for comparison only. Many high-school graduates will possess much of the needed knowledge, as will many men who have studied refrigeration and air-conditioning theory and practice and are now working in this field. From a high-school education, or from an equivalent informal educational program, it is an easy step to a public or private trade-technical school that offers two-year college-level courses in Refrigeration and/or Air-Conditioning Technology.

BASIC EDUCATION

1. *Arithmetic and Vocational Mathematics.* All of the experts consulted were in agreement on the need for a good working knowledge of arithmetic and vocational mathematics. This knowledge should include the use of formulas and constants that are commonly used in heat-load calculations, areas of surfaces, contents of tanks, insulating factors, and other elements used in cost estimating in the refrigeration business, plus the simpler applications of algebra and geometry.

2. *Applied Physics and Chemistry.* Every technician, mechanic, operating engineer, and plant engineer in the refrigeration and air-conditioning industry should have some knowledge of the chemicals used for water softening, cleaning compounds, brine and eutectic solutions, oils, greases, and other substances commonly used in the operation and care of heating, ventilating,

BASIC EDUCATIONAL REQUIREMENTS 33

refrigeration, air-conditioning, and other mechanical systems. To this should be added some knowledge of the properties of refrigerants, measurement of heat, fundamentals of electricity, magnetism, strength of materials, etc.

3. *Safety.* Safety is probably the single most important factor in the operation and care of any heating, ventilating, refrigeration, and air-conditioning plant, or other mechanical system used in modern buildings. One of the most important elements involved in safety is good housekeeping, and every mechanic, technician, operator, and plant engineer is responsible for the maintenance of clean, orderly, and safe workshops, storage areas, and machinery rooms. These men must understand the action and reaction of refrigerants, industrial gases, and other chemicals when they are exposed to extremes of temperature and pressure such as might result from fire.

4. *Spare Parts, Supplies, Tools, and Fuel.* On most jobs the technicians, mechanics, and plant engineers have the responsibility for ordering spare parts, supplies, tools, fuel, and replacement equipment for all mechanical systems in the buildings under their care. They are expected to anticipate the needs of their department and to place orders well in advance of actual need. They must also develop a system for the safe, clean, and orderly storage of such supplies and equipment. In most instances they do not have the responsibility for the actual purchase, but they must master the system of purchase orders and requisitions used by the purchasing department. Every technical training program should give some attention to the use of catalogs, order forms, and requisition procedures. Such knowledge can be an important factor when men are up for promotion.

5. *Records, Charts, Day Books, and Logs.* Every technician, mechanic, operating engineer, and plant engineer is responsible for keeping charts, records, and logs of plant operation, repairs, maintenance, and departmental activities. Such records might include a Day Book to record tasks assigned and accomplished, service calls, maintenance, and department needs. The operating engineers must keep a regular log of plant tem-

peratures and pressures, humidity readings, fuel consumption, etc. The chief engineer must have knowledge of office procedures, employee/employer relationships, employee benefits, time keeping, shift schedules, hiring and firing policies, and elements of effective supervision.

Much of the knowledge and experience needed to hold a good job in the heating and air-conditioning industry can be acquired in school and in on-the-job training. However, no trade-technical school program will supply all of the answers. A great deal of the knowledge and information needed must be acquired by applying common sense to the routine tasks and problems that are encountered in day-to-day school and work activities.

Probably the most important step to be taken by any man who aims at a career in this field is to select the general branch of the industry in which he would like to specialize, and then direct all effort to the accomplishment of this goal. The basic and technical educational requirements are much the same for all branches of the refrigeration and air-conditioning sales, installation, operation, and service field. To select a specialty does not mean that a man must stress one occupational field above all others, nor does it mean a blind and inflexible commitment to any field. Every technical training program should be subject to adjustment as need arises.

TECHNICAL EDUCATIONAL REQUIREMENTS

For many years the best entry into a good job or an independent business in refrigeration and air-conditioning sales, installation, and service was by means of a formal apprenticeship in one of the trades of the field. Under this arrangement a man would spend from four to five years in a program that included classroom work and on-the-job training. This is a proven method for producing qualified technicians and mechanics, but the current opportunities for a formal apprenticeship in this field are rather limited.

BASIC EDUCATIONAL REQUIREMENTS

This circumstance has made it necessary for many men who want to qualify for a good job in refrigeration and air conditioning to turn to what might be considered the rough equivalent of a formal apprenticeship—an informal apprenticeship. Under this system the student-worker must find his own jobs and obtain whatever basic and technical education he can by his own efforts.

The refrigeration and air-conditioning industry has been expanding since the day it was established, and its technology changes from month to month. However, many of these changes are concerned with applications of equipment, and the fundamental technical knowledge required stays much the same. For this reason, it is essential for the technician or mechanic to acquire, at the beginning of his career, a sound basic and technical education. With this background it will be easy to adapt to new developments as they appear.

Since the chances for a formal apprenticeship are not good, it is possible that the best entry into the field would be through one of the two-year courses in Refrigeration and/or Air-Conditioning Technology that are offered by many public and private trade-technical schools.

It should be noted, however, that the man who takes this method of entry to a job in refrigeration and air conditioning will not, at the completion of his two-year college education, be in the same position as the man who has come into the field through a formal apprenticeship—though his lifetime earning potential may be higher.

The student who has earned an Associate in Science degree in Refrigeration and/or Air-Conditioning Technology will be in much the same position as any college graduate—he will have to serve a period of internship in order to gain the practical experience that will make him valuable to his employer.

Trade-technical school records prove that a man who has an Associate Degree in the field is in immediate demand by employers who hire engineering assistants, sales engineers, draftsmen, estimators, building engineers, plant engineers, field

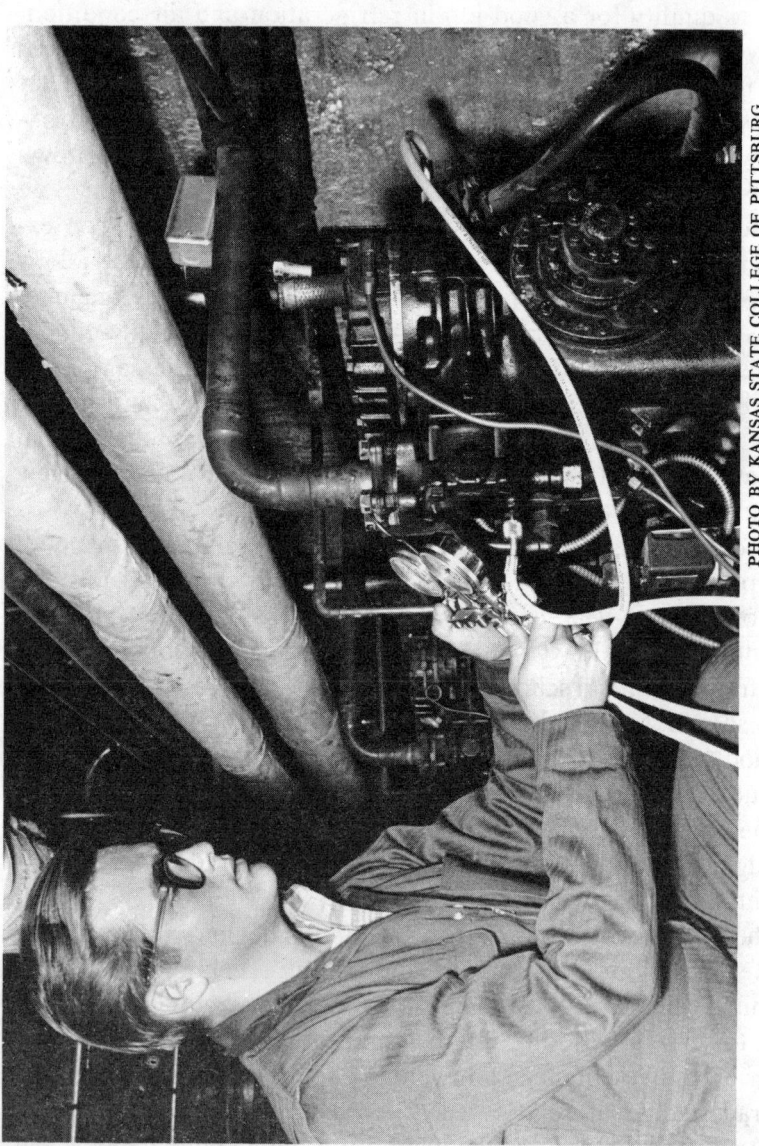

PHOTO BY KANSAS STATE COLLEGE OF PITTSBURG

The Vocational Technical Institute at Kansas State College uses all of the refrigeration and air-conditioning equipment of the 5,000-student campus as training aids. In this manner students are able, after months of training, to meet their "moment of truth."

service managers, erectors, and many others. If none of these jobs sounds attractive there is always the opportunity to establish an independent dealer-contractor business.

An additional plus factor in having completed the two-year college-level education that should be given very serious consideration is the possibility that a student might want to extend his education. A man who has earned an Associate in Science degree by his own efforts has demonstrated qualities that are admired by all employers. If, after a year or two of field experience, this man decides to go back to school and work for a degree in refrigeration and air-conditioning engineering, or mechanical engineering, the chances are good that his employer would subsidize a part of the cost.

The following list of courses for an Associate in Science degree in Air-Conditioning Technology have been taken from the catalog of a trade-technical college that has offered training in this subject for more than thirty years. At the present time this school offers fifty-two courses in refrigeration and air-conditioning technology and techniques. A selection from this number of courses can be made to suit the technical training needs of any student, in any stage of development, and for any occupational field within this industry.

The course of study outlined is rather strongly oriented to the engineering level and the new job opportunities in the refrigeration and air-conditioning sales, installation, service, and operation fields. The outlines offered here are for comparison purposes only. If the student wants to prepare for a job in another occupational field within this industry, the course of study should be adjusted to the requirements of that field.

AIR-CONDITIONING TECHNOLOGY
ASSOCIATE IN SCIENCE DEGREE CURRICULUM

The requirements for an Associate in Science degree in Air-Conditioning Technology may be met by completing the essential courses listed here, and sufficient electives to meet the sixty-unit requirement. The recommended electives may be substituted for courses in the Air-Conditioning Technology major with the approval of the Department Coordinator. All students must complete one or more of the required academic courses each semester, to be taken concurrently with the Air-Conditioning Technology major, as scheduled by the Department Coordinator.

(*Note:* Courses marked with an asterisk carry one unit of credit for each eighteen hours of work completed. Courses not so designated are evaluated on the basis of sixty hours of work being equivalent to one unit. Figures in parentheses following Course Heading indicate units).

1. *Orientation to Air Conditioning** (1): The course offers a brief history of the industry including present-day conditions and practices, employment information, and the role of the technician in this field.

2. *Heating and Ventilating Theory and Practice** (2): Fundamentals of heating and ventilating, heat-load calculations, gas-fired heating equipment, and forced-air systems are studied.

3. *Heating and Ventilating Practice* (1): Laboratory course familiarizes student with heating and ventilating equipment, and provides instruction in measurement of the performance of heating and combustion equipment.

4. *Thermal and Instrumentation Laboratory* (1): Provides instruction in the use of measuring instruments common in the industry. Principles of heating, heat balance, heat transfer, combustion, and ventilating are demonstrated.

5. *Applied Physics I* (2): Instruction is provided in the area of precision measurement of heat.

6. *Applied Statistics and Strength of Materials* (1): Principles and practices relating to forces, moments, friction, properties of materials, riveted and welded joints, and shafts are studied.

7. *Mathematics for Air Conditioning I** (2): Fundamental mathematics is offered as it applies to heating, including problem-solving practice with applicable formulas.

BASIC EDUCATIONAL REQUIREMENTS 39

8. *Basic Drafting for Air Conditioning I* (1): Instruction is offered in the basic principles and practices of drafting, lettering, geometrical solutions, views, and projections.

9. *Applied Chemistry for Air Conditioning* (1): Principles relating to water hardness and treatment, corrosion, eutectic solutions and brines, refrigerant testing for moisture and acid, compressor oil test, and combustion are studied.

10. *Air-Conditioning System Installation Practice and Methods* (2): Instruction is provided in sheet metal fabrication, pipe jointing, methods and installation practices, welding, and plumbing.

11. *Basic Electrical Theory** (2): Electricity and magnetism, D.C. and A.C. circuits and machines, measuring instruments, electrical distribution, and utilization practices are studied.

12. *Applied Electricity* (1): Electrical system components, A.C. circuits, branch wiring, magnetic starters, and relays are studied in the laboratory.

13. *Refrigeration Cycle Principles** (2): Fundamentals of mechanical refrigeration, properties of refrigerants, heat pumps, and systems' performance calculations are studied.

14. *Refrigeration Cycle Applications* (1): Laboratory course offers evaluation of equipment performance, heat balance, and determination of coefficient of performance and operating cycles.

15. *Advanced Refrigeration Principles** (2): Instruction is offered in the area of absorption and centrifugal and air-cycle refrigeration, as well as cryogenics.

16. *Advanced Drafting for Air Conditioning* (1): Practice is offered in developments and intersections, and in symbols; layouts for heating and air conditioning are made.

17. *Psychrometrics** (2): Course examines the properties of moist air and the interpretation of air-conditioning processes on the psychrometric chart.

18. *Mathematics for Air Conditioning II** (2): Covers applied mathematics, comprising elements of algebra, geometry, and logarithms.

19. *Applied Drafting I for Air Conditioning* (2): Instruction is offered in layout and drafting of air-conditioning and heating systems for residential applications.

20. *Heat Gain Theory** (2): Theory and practice of calculating loads for air conditioning, including short-form methods, are studied.

21. *Air-Distribution Principles** (2): Requirements for good air distribution, outlet performance, volume control, noise limitation, and selection and location of outlets are studied.

22. *Air Distribution* (1): Laboratory demonstrations are made of outlet performance, use of air-flow measuring devices, and system balancing.

23. *Equipment Selection Theory** (2): Instruction is given in the use of manufacturers' catalogs to select and size such equipment as air-handling units, coils, cooling towers, condensing units, fans, and pumps.

24. *Applied Equipment Selection* (1): Laboratory projects are designed to demonstrate the performance of equipment, both separately and as an integral part of commercial and residential systems.

25. *Applied Drafting II for Air Conditioning* (1): Students complete projects in the layout and drafting of air-conditioning systems for residential or small commercial applications.

26. *Applied Physics II* (2): Instruction is provided in the areas of mechanics, heat, electricity, and magnetism.

27. *Air Conditioning Control Theory** (1): Fundamental control theory, electrical and pneumatic controls, and current practices regarding application to refrigeration equipment, residential and commercial systems are studied.

28. *Air Conditioning Control Application* (2): This laboratory course investigates the practical application of control devices.

29. *Hydronics Theory and Practice** (2): Instruction includes the study of fluid flow, pumps and pumping, boilers, forced circulation, hot-water heating, water chillers, and chilled-water circulating systems.

BASIC EDUCATIONAL REQUIREMENTS 41

30. *Hydronics Applications* (1): Laboratory course includes instruction in measurement of fluid flow, and performance of chilled- and hot-water systems, including components such as pumps and coils.

31. *Cost Estimating for Air Conditioning** (2): Methods and procedures in cost estimating for heating and air-conditioning projects are explored.

The thirty-one courses listed here have a total weight of forty-eight units. The remaining courses to make up a total of sixty, required to earn an Associate in Science degree in Air-Conditioning Technology, must be approved academic courses.

Not all trade-technical schools offer the variety of courses outlined in this chapter, but any training program should include most of these subjects. Most schools will adjust the courses in a curriculum to meet the requirements of the occupational field selected by the student. In addition, most schools will give credit for work already completed, allowing the student to broaden his technical study background.

To illustrate how required subjects may be substituted for courses in the air-conditioning technology major, the following elective courses are permitted by this school. This group of courses would be of value to the student who expected to seek a job in the installation, service, operation, and maintenance field, rather than in engineering occupations.

RECOMMENDED ELECTIVE COURSES

36. *Air Conditioning** (3): This course is intended to assist the mechanic, technician, estimator, or salesman in understanding the theory behind the installation and the equipment necessary to the system. It is a design course that includes the study of heat and energy, psychrometrics, airflow, equipment, and controls.

37. *Refrigeration and Air Conditioning I ** (3): This course is offered for journeymen and refrigeration mechanics who desire additional technical information concerning refrigeration

systems. Instruction is given in refrigerant properties, refrigeration cycle controls, evaporators, condensers, pumps, compressors, piping, and fittings.

38. *Refrigeration and Air Conditioning II* * (3): Instruction includes refrigeration and air-conditioning systems, air handling, installations, motors, safety, and relations on the job.

42. *Heating and Air Conditioning I* * (3): Basic instruction is given for workmen in the heating and air-conditioning field. The course covers heating, fundamentals of fuels, venting, heat-transfer calculations, equipment selection, distribution systems, and necessary controls.

43. *Heating and Air Conditioning II* * (3): This course offers specialized study of the cooling sector of the air-conditioning field for employed mechanics. A study is made of the types of systems, refrigeration cycle, heat gain and calculation, air-distribution equipment, selection of controls, and sales procedures.

45. *Refrigeration and Air-Conditioning Electricity** (3): This course is designed to provide the journeyman mechanic and technician with a basic knowledge of electricity. It includes fundamental theory, electrical equipment used in air-conditioning circuits, and wiring practices. Electricity as applied to temperature and refrigeration controls is stressed.

46. *Heating, Ventilation, and Refrigeration Code** (3): This course offers instruction in the local codes and ordinances for the heating, ventilating, and refrigeration trades. Students study the regulations concerning safety, public health, design and construction of equipment installations, and the operation and maintenance of heating, ventilating, refrigeration, and air-conditioning equipment.

CHAPTER IV

The Best Job for You

The selection of the right job, and the best field of opportunity, in refrigeration and air conditioning is made difficult by the fact that this is a fragmented industry with many branches. These special branches are not closely related; each goes its own way and is concerned only with its own problems. The situation is further complicated because comprehensive counseling is not always available and it is not possible to obtain information that will give a clear picture of each field of opportunity.

Before any problem can be solved, it is necessary to define that problem and to discover the elements that make it a problem. In the case of refrigeration and air conditioning the problem is to select the job that will offer the best chance to establish a rewarding career. To do this it is necessary to examine the education, technical training, experience, and duties of many jobs—in other words, to compile a sort of "score card" outlining the requirements of each field and each job.

Fortunately, there is a wealth of material available that can be used to compile that "score card." It is contained in a series of *Job Bulletins,* which have been prepared by city, county, state, and federal civil service commissions and by personnel managers in many industries. These bulletins offer jobs ranging from that of a semiskilled maintenance man who performs routine repair and maintenance tasks, to that of a top-level supervisor who is responsible for all of the mechanical equipment in an entire complex of buildings.

The information on jobs presented here has been taken from actual Job Bulletins, but to save space details have been deleted. For full information on civil service jobs the applicant should inquire at the agency. For information on jobs in industry apply at the personnel department of any business that uses men in this category.

MODERN PRIVATE AND PUBLIC BUILDINGS

The development of new civic centers, convention facilities, sports arenas, office buildings, hotels, and shopping centers, all of which have the latest machinery and systems for heating, ventilating, refrigeration, and air conditioning, has meant many fine job opportunities for refrigeration and air-conditioning mechanics and technicians, operating engineers, building engineers, and building superintendents. However, this growth has also brought many problems to the personnel managers and hiring agencies who must recruit qualified men to service, maintain, and operate these complex mechanical systems, including refrigeration and air conditioning.

The old buildings that are being replaced by these modern structures often had heating, ventilating, refrigeration, and air-conditioning plants that were rather primitive, by modern standards. The men who were responsible for the maintenance and operation of these older plants did not, in many instances, have the technical training, experience, and skill needed to manage these more complex mechanical systems. Employers often found it necessary to turn to other fields to recruit men with the needed qualifications.

This method of hiring skilled workers was effective for a time, but as more and more large civic centers and private buildings were built, the competition for qualified men increased. It soon became obvious that special training programs would have to be developed, but trade-technical schools were slow to respond to this need. However, there are now indications that this training void is being filled, and some very good technical training programs are now available.

The four jobs outlined in this section do not cover the full range of jobs in this field, but they are typical and they set out

PHOTO BY HONEYWELL

Master control console enables operator to keep tabs on all four buildings of the Occidental Center complex; by simply touching pushbuttons he can control mechanical equipment in the next room or thirty-four stories above. The TV-like screen in front of the operator projects schematic drawings of various mechanical systems; pushbuttons are electronically tied into that same system. Three gauges above the screen are linked to instruments on a rooftop helicopter landing pad; the console also watches over elevators, waterfalls, exterior lighting on building, fuel supply, and FM radio transmitter on the roof.

in detail the education, training, experience, and duties of this field. Probably the best time to apply for such jobs would be while the building or buildings are under construction.

Chief Engineer
Work level—Supervisory. Salary $13,500 to $18,500 per year. Duties—Plan, assign, and supervise the work of semi-skilled and skilled workers in the operation, maintenance, and repair of heating, ventilating, refrigeration, air-conditioning, electrical, and other mechanical systems in a large building or group of buildings. Will be responsible for the care of stationary engines, boilers, compressors, pumps, cooling towers, evaporative coolers, condensers, steam lines, water lines, and other piping-system components.

Experience Requirements—Substantial; to be established by application, investigation, and interviews.

Office-Building Engineer
Work level—Technical and Supervisory. Salary $12,000 to $15,000. Duties—Under direction, to operate, maintain, and repair low-pressure boilers and heating systems, refrigeration, ventilation, and air-conditioning equipment, and other mechanical systems. Inspect and report on the condition of air, gas, water, and refrigerant piping throughout the building. Make emergency repairs and adjustments as needed.

Experience Requirements—One year of experience performing the duties of a stationary fireman in a building having equivalent mechanical equipment. Two years of experience in the operation, maintenance, and repair of such equipment. (Completion of a two-year college-level course in Air-Conditioning Technology may be substituted for one year of the required experience.)

Refrigeration and Air-Conditioning Mechanic
Work level—Journeyman. Salary $12,500 to $14,800 per year. Duties—Performs journeyman-level installation, maintenance,

PHOTO BY AIR CONDITIONING, HEATING & REFRIGERATION NEWS

When the operator in the control room pushes the buttons, this is where much of the action takes place. This is the mechanical equipment room for a large hospital. Air-conditioning equipment by Carrier.

and repairs on heating, ventilating, refrigeration, and air-conditioning equipment and related components. Diagnoses trouble and makes repairs or replaces associated mechanisms as required. Performs minor and major overhaul of refrigeration and air-conditioning equipment and makes operational tests of equipment. Prepares progress and operating reports; keeps a Log or Day Book and orders spare parts and supplies as needed.

Experience Requirements—Applicants must have completed an apprenticeship in this trade, or have had work experience to be the substantial equivalent of a completed apprenticeship. Mechanics should be able to perform duties of the job with no more than normal supervision. May be required to supervise the work of skilled and semiskilled workers in the cleaning, overhaul, and maintenance of refrigeration, air-conditioning, heating, and related equipment.

Auditorium or Sports Arena Engineer

Work level—Technical and Supervisory. Salary $13,600 to $17,000. Duties—This is a technical and supervisory job in plant operation and building maintenance at a convention center in a city of approximately 100,000 population. Work involves supervision of maintenance and operation of refrigeration and air-conditioning equipment, boilers, heating, ventilating, and electrical systems, ice-making equipment for the skating rink, kitchen equipment (catering only). The engineer has overall supervision over building cleaning and building maintenance and assigns routine and special tasks to subordinates. He recruits, trains, and supervises labor for setting up and tearing down special-events layouts as required by the renters.

Experience Requirements—Qualifications for jobs in this class are often established by job applications, experience résumés, interviews, investigation, and examination. Quality of experience, where the applicant has shown the ability to assume responsibility, may carry more weight than experience that called for routine activities. Reference to the completion of a two-year college-level course in Refrigeration and Air-Conditioning Technology is found in many such Job Bulletins.

The development of a new type of building that combines the features of an auditorium, convention center, and sports arena has opened up an entirely new field of job opportunities for refrigeration and air-conditioning technicians, mechanics, and operating engineers. Some of these new facilities are owned and operated by a city or county agency, but most are under private ownership.

All buildings of this type have extensive mechanical installations, and the operation, maintenance, repair, and cleaning of the building and grounds are the responsibility of the building superintendent. The maintenance, cleaning, and operating crews consist of one or more engineers, technicians, mechanics, and other skilled and semiskilled workers.

The mechanical systems in these buildings, including the refrigeration and air-conditioning equipment, represent an investment of hundreds of thousands of dollars. For this reason employers often turn to men who have had substantial experience in the care and operation of such equipment to fill jobs on every level from operating engineer to building superintendent. More and more often the Job Bulletins for such jobs include the following condition—"Completion of a two-year college-level course in Refrigeration and Air Conditioning Technology, which must have included the actual operation of steam boilers and modern multi-zone air-conditioning systems, may be substituted for one year of the required experience."

SEMISKILLED JOBS

As we have seen, only a limited number of formal apprenticeships are available in the refrigeration and air-conditioning sales, installation, service, and operating field, and not all men are able to complete a college-level course in Refrigeration and Air-Conditioning Technology, but these are not the only means of entry into a good job in this industry.

In the past it was the policy of many employers, in both private and public buildings, to draw a rather clear-cut line between the men who were responsible for the cleaning of buildings and grounds and those who were responsible for the maintenance, repair, and operation of mechanical equipment. In recent years this line has not been so clearly drawn, and many employers now try to hire semskilled workers who have the ability and the ambition to advance to more responsible jobs.

If an ambitious man understands the problem and elects to enter the building maintenance field through a semiskilled job, he does not necessarily have to remain on that level for many years. On the contrary, there is an ever-growing need for qualified men to fill jobs in the new buildings, and employers are always looking for candidates who can be developed by on-the-job training and company-sponsored technical educational programs. In many instances the training programs use a combination of local trade-technical and home-study courses. The two jobs outlined here do not mark the limits of opportunities in this field, but they are typical.

Building Maintenanceman

Work level—Semiskilled. Salary $9,000 to $11,700 per year. Duties—Under supervision, to do general custodial and light maintenance work in the upkeep of large buildings. Assignments might include repair or replacement of lighting-system components, doors, door locks, and similar tasks calling for handyman skills; general cleaning of public areas; and setting up or removing facilities, desks, cabinets, etc. Duties may involve some leadman activities when temporary employees are hired for special events in the auditorium and meeting rooms.

Experience Requirements—Completion of the tenth school grade and some experience in maintenance and janitorial work. Must have ability to carry out oral or written instructions and to perform routine tasks without close supervision. Will be required to use hand tools and operate small tractors, fork lifts, and power-cleaning equipment.

Building Maintenance Foreman
Work level—Supervisory. Salary $12,000 to $16,000 per year. Duties—Supervisory work in the care and general maintenance of a large building, or group of buildings. The foreman supervises, and may participate in, the work of subordinates. All work is performed under the supervision of the building engineer or building superintendent. Maintenance foreman must have some knowledge of operation of low-pressure boilers, heating, ventilating, refrigeration, and air-conditioning equipment and components; considerable knowledge of methods, practices, tools, and materials used in this type of work. Must have good knowledge of occupational hazards and safety precautions applicable to building cleaning and maintenance.

Experience Requirements—Graduation from a standard high school or vocational school, and several years of experience in this field. The ability to plan, lay out work, and supervise subordinates in a manner conducive to full performance and good morale. (Many job openings in this field are promotional.)

STATIONARY FIREMEN & OPERATING ENGINEERS

Nearly all of the new buildings that have a large central mechanical plant have high-pressure boilers to provide steam for heating systems and for hot water for domestic use. These boilers are in operation twenty-four hours a day 365 days a year. In many states high-pressure boilers must be under the care of a licensed fireman or engineer. Every building or complex of buildings has at least one fireman or engineer on each shift. With a relief engineer, this means a minimum of four jobs in each plant of this type.

Stationary Engineer or Fireman
Work level—Operator (shift work). Salary $11,700 to $14,400. Duties—Supervise the operation of high-pressure boiler systems; operate, maintain, and adjust heating, lighting, refrigeration, air-conditioning, and ventilating equipment. Inspect, repair, and

report on the condition of mechanical equipment throughout the building. Keep charts and records and make written reports.

Experience Requirements—One year of experience in performing the duties of a stationary fireman or engineer in a large building or institution, or equivalent experience in industry or business. Two years of full-time experience in the operation and care of high-pressure boiler systems, heating systems, and related mechanical equipment. (Completion of a two-year college-level course in Air-Conditioning Technology, which must have included the actual operation of high-pressure boilers and multi-zone air-conditioning systems, may be substituted for one year of the required experience.)

Note: The jobs outlined in this section are more closely related to heating and air conditioning than to refrigeration. For this reason, the man who seeks a job in this field should stress Air-Conditioning Technology in his technical education.

CHAPTER V

Cold Storage and Institutional Refrigeration

Cold storage and institutional refrigeration has not been as widely publicized as some branches of this industry, but it is an expanding field and offers fine job opportunities for men who have the right education, technical training, and experience. Job classifications range from a refrigeration plant operator with a salary of $12,000 to $14,500 per year to a plant superintendent at from $12,000 to $20,000 per year.

Many jobs in cold storage and institutional refrigeration are offered by city, county, state, and federal civil service commissions and are concerned with the management, operation, maintenance, and service of refrigeration and air-conditioning plants in public institutions such as hospitals, colleges, and penal institutions. Equivalent jobs exist in every business and industry that involves cold storage, food processing, meat packing, and many other on-farm and off-farm activities that require refrigeration. However, the largest and fastest-growing segment of this industry is in the storage and distribution terminals that are operated for, and in conjunction with, air, rail, truck, and marine cold-storage terminals and distribution facilities.

The information presented here has been taken from Job Bulletins that have offered jobs in this field. It does not cover the full range of such jobs, but the examples are typical and set out in rather clear terms the education, training, and experience requirements. Full information can be obtained at any civil service commission or personnel department.

Plant Engineer
Work level—Supervisory. Salary $12,750 to $16,000 per year. Duties—Plans, assigns, and supervises the work of skilled, semi-

PHOTO BY AIR CONDITIONING, HEATING & REFRIGERATION NEWS

In this photo an operating engineer records pressures and temperatures for a cold-storage plant. Cold storage and food distribution are often taken for granted, but they represent one of the most complex and fastest-growing branches of the refrigeration industry.

skilled, and inmate helpers (institution only) in the operation, maintenance, and repair of heating, ventilating, air-conditioning, refrigeration and cold-storage equipment, including stationary engines, boilers, compressors, pumps, and condensers; water, steam, and gas lines and piping; and fire protection and safety equipment. Evaluates staff performance and takes or recommends appropriate action. Prepares requisitions for fuel equipment, spare parts, and supplies and is responsible for clean and orderly storage of such items. Keeps, or directs the keeping of, charts and records and prepares written reports as needed.

Experience Requirements—Two full years of recent experience in the maintenance and operation of large modern heating, ventilating, air-conditioning, refrigeration, and cold-storage systems of the type found in large commercial, industrial, or governmental institutions and buildings. He must have general knowledge of state safety orders and industrial safety regulations that apply to the operation of extensive mechanical systems. He must be familiar with the principles of effective supervision.

Refrigeration Engineman

Work level—Operator (shift work). Salary $12,000 to $14,500. Duties—Under direction, operates and cares for mechanical equipment used for refrigeration and cold storage of food and other goods. Work includes operation of refrigerating compressors, brine pumps, circulating water pumps, evaporative condensers, blowers, fans, control valves, and other components of a large mechanical refrigeration system. Makes repairs as needed, checks and regulates temperature, humidity, and forced-air circulation to meet the requirements of goods in storage; reads and logs temperatures, pressures, and humidity readings and keeps a Day Book of plant activities.

Experience Requirements—Completion of the twelfth school grade and three years of experience in the operation of mechanical refrigeration systems of not less than 100 tons of refrigerating capacity per twenty-four hours. Must be able to read and work from plans, drawings, and mechanical or construction specifica-

PHOTO BY AIR CONDITIONING, HEATING & REFRIGERATION NEWS

The cooling tower is an important component of many refrigeration and air-conditioning installations. Water treatment, water conditioning, and water testing are carried out on a daily schedule, and this work is included in the duties of most operating engineers, mechanics, and building engineers.

tions. May be required to supervise the work of skilled and semi-skilled workers in plant maintenance and overhaul; must think and act quickly in emergencies.

Refrigeration Mechanic
Work level—Journeyman. Salary $14,000 to $16,500 per year. Duties—Installs refrigeration components such as compressors, evaporators, condensers, motors, pumps, fans, blowers, etc. Installs and connects piping, fittings, and tubing for refrigeration and air-conditioning equipment; calibrates and repairs refrigeration plant controls. Diagnoses operating malfunctions and makes needed repairs and adjustments. Tests, charges, repairs, and adjusts hermetic type refrigeration units, self-contained refrigeration units, ammonia ice and refrigeration plants, and brine refrigeration systems. Supervises the work of helpers and apprentices. Must have valid driver's license.

Experience Requirements—Completion of a recognized refrigeration mechanic apprentice training program of at least five years' duration, or six years of experience in the installation, alteration, maintenance, and repair of commercial, industrial, and domestic refrigeration and air-conditioning units and systems. One year of this experience must have been on the journeyman level and must include experience in the installation, operation, and maintenance of large multi-zone air-conditioning systems.

Readers may be surprised to learn that the pay rate for a journeyman-level job is higher, in some instances, than that for a stationary engineer, operating engineer, or plant engineer. However, the reasons become obvious when the training and experience requirements for these jobs are compared. Many top-level supervisory jobs in this field are filled from the journeyman level. Probably the next best preparation for a job in this field would be a two-year college course in Refrigeration Technology.

For the man who must prepare for such jobs by means of an informal apprenticeship of home study, trade school, and on-the-job training, it would be wise to include the following elements. Course outlines have been taken from the catalog of a larger trade-technical school and are a part of the Refrigeration Technology major.

7. *Food Industry Refrigeration I* * (3): Cold storage is studied with emphasis on heat-load calculations, design temperatures, insulation factors, and equipment sizing.

8. *Food Industry Refrigeration II* * (3): This course covers the advanced aspects of general food preservation, including theory of ripening, enzymic action, and heat of aspiration.

9. *Food Industry Refrigeration III* * (3): This course includes heat-gain calculations, low-temperature food storage requirements, quick freezing, humidity, and effects of evaporator temperature; defrost methods are also studied.

10. *Refrigeration for Liquid Cooling** (3): Refrigeration applications to beverage cooling, beer coolers, milk coolers, breweries, and special requirements in wine processing, as well as applications using secondary refrigerants, are studied.

21. *Refrigeration Operation Procedures* (1): Students gain practical shop experience in units and system operation. Emphasis is placed on economy, maintenance of temperatures, log keeping, safety, and housekeeping.

Note: Courses marked with an asterisk require eighteen hours of work for each unit of credit. Courses not so marked require sixty hours of work for each unit of credit.

CHAPTER VI

Marine Refrigeration

Marine refrigeration and air conditioning is one of the most fascinating branches of the industry, and men who live in an area where there are shipbuilding and ship repair facilities should not overlook the job opportunities in this field.

The United States does not have a large merchant marine, and many of its merchant ships are built in foreign yards, but the U.S. Navy, Coast Guard, and Army operate every type of water transport vehicle, from atomic-powered aircraft carrier to motorized scow. Each of these ships or boats, if it carries perishable cargo or has a crew living aboard, must have mechanical refrigeration for the preservation of food and other perishables and for air conditioning of office and living space.

The information presented here for a journeyman-level job was taken from a Job Bulletin circulated by a U.S. Naval Shipyard. However, the education, technical training, and experience requirements would be identical for jobs in privately owned shipyards, boatyards, and repair facilities. This field also offers many jobs for helpers, apprentices, journeymen, and supervisors. Most supervisory jobs are filled from the journeyman level by means of promotional examinations in U.S. government facilities, and on the basis of merit and seniority in private facilities.

Refrigeration Mechanic
Work level—Journeyman. Pay rate $5.45 to $5.95 per hour. Duties—Working from blueprints and under direction, installs, maintains, and repairs refrigeration and air-conditioning equipment and components used for living quarters, public areas, and industrial cold storage.

PHOTO BY MATSON LINES

Food and other perishable products are brought to market by every conceivable type of transportation. In this photo the Matson Lines container and refrigerated cargo ship Hawaiian Citizen is fully loaded and headed for the mainland.

MARINE REFRIGERATION

Experience Requirements—Applicants must have completed a four-year apprenticeship in the trade, or have had practical experience to be the substantial equivalent of a completed apprenticeship. This experience must include, or have been supplemented by, at least six months of experience in operation and service on modern multi-zone air-conditioning equipment. Experience should include the layout, fabrication, and installation of refrigeration piping and tubing; the use of freon refrigerants; the installation and repair of compressors, evaporators, and coils; the installation of electric motors, fans, and blowers. Other duties might include pipe bending, tube bending, silver brazing (soldering), hand cutting and threading of pipe, etc.

Substitution—Well-rounded experience in industrial pipefitting may be substituted, on a month-for-month basis, for up to two years of the required experience.

EQUIVALENT JOBS IN BUSINESS AND INDUSTRY

The qualifications for jobs in refrigeration and air conditioning in a naval shipyard or repair facility also apply to jobs in private industry. There are four chief classes of shipbuilding and ship repair work, for both private and governmental yards:

1. The building of new ships and boats.
2. The conversion of existing ships and boats to another class of service.
3. Major overhaul of ships and boats in service.
4. Voyage repairs usually of an emergency nature and done while a ship is in port for discharge or loading of cargo and passengers.

CONTAINERIZATION

The use of containers for the shipment of perishable products is a fairly new development in marine refrigeration that is growing at a very rapid rate. The shipping container is an insulated box that can be loaded at a distant point and hauled to the dock by air, truck, or rail. These containers have not been standardized, but a popular size is approximately 8 ft. wide × 8 ft. high × 35 ft. in length. Refrigerated containers use a mechanical refrigeration unit similar to those used for truck and trailer bodies. Nonmechanical refrigerating systems are also used.

FISHING INDUSTRY

Before World War II most fishing boats and tuna clippers that operated offshore were limited in range by the amount of ice they could load in the hold. If the ice melted before fish were found, the boats had to return to port with empty tanks. Mechanical refrigeration greatly increased the range of these boats, and they could stay at sea for weeks if need be. Boats of this type are to be found in any port where offshore fishing fleets operate.

Probably the best way to prepare for a journeyman-level job in marine refrigeration would be through a four- to five-year formal apprenticeship, but this avenue is closed to many men. Fortunately, work experience gained in other branches of refrigeration and air conditioning, and related fields, is recognized by many employers. This makes it feasible to acquire the needed training and experience by means of trade-technical school studies and on-the-job experience. The standard Refrigeration and Air-Conditioning Technology subjects should be studied, but special emphasis should be placed on the following elements.

18. *Refrigeration Servicing Procedures II* (2): Variations from normal operating conditions are observed in the laboratory and remedial service procedures performed. Check-test-and-start practices for systems above *five tons'* capacity are practiced.

37. *Refrigeration and Air Conditioning I* (3): This course is offered for journeymen and technicians who desire additional technical information concerning refrigeration systems. Instruction is given in refrigerant properties, refrigeration cycle con-

Two cranes load containers on the S.S. Californian at the Alameda, California, container yard. The use of containers has reduced the number of men and the time required for loading ships. Containers can be used for either dry cargo or products requiring refrigeration.

PHOTO BY MATSON LINES

trols, evaporators, condensers, pumps, compressors, piping, and fitting.

39. *Refrigeration and Air-Conditioning Controls* (3): This course is open to refrigeration mechanics and technicians only, and its purpose is to help these men understand the various types of controls for refrigeration and air-conditioning systems. The course includes fundamental principles of electric circuits and pneumatic circuits, installation problems, and service and maintenance problems.

40. *Refrigeration Welding and Silver Brazing* (1): This course is offered to supplement the mechanic's skill in silver brazing and soldering. It covers technical terms, torches, fluxes, metal alloys, brazing rules, practice in making brazed joints, and testing of completed work.

CHAPTER VII

Automotive Air Conditioning and Transport Refrigeration

Modern automotive air conditioning got its start shortly after World War II when enterprising individuals built mechanical refrigeration units from conventional components and mounted them in the trunk compartments of passenger cars. These units filled the trunk area, and the air-circulation system called for extensive penetrations through the inner body of the car. The controls were rather primitive, but the system did work.

As demand developed, engineers designed units that could be adapted to any make or model of car, and production skyrocketed. At the present time automotive air conditioning is, in terms of the number of new units sold each year, the fastest-growing branch of the refrigeration industry. Some authorities place the number of units currently in service at 30,000,000, and if present production rates continue, this number could triple within ten years.

Automotive air conditioning is considered an accessory, and sales, installation, and service of this equipment are more closely related to the automobile industry than to refrigeration and air conditioning. Most of the mechanics who specialize in this field have been drawn from the ranks of automotive service men and mechanics. The installation and service of automotive air conditioning has not been classified as a skilled trade. In fact, many shop owners believe they can teach any man who has some mechanical aptitude all he needs to know in one week. Obviously, however, a service man with this limited amount of training and experience would have to work under very close supervision.

Automotive air-conditioning equipment manufacturers are now combining the heating and cooling system into a single unit with a more complex control system. These installations will be more difficult to install, service, and maintain, and there are now indications that limited-skill mechanics will no longer serve the needs of the industry. Training programs are being extended to produce the qualified technicians who will be in demand in the near future.

Automotive air conditioning has always been a very seasonal activity; up to 80 percent of all service work is done in the period between May 15 and September 15. For this reason, the field has had little attraction as a full-time career, except for men who hoped to become a service manager in a large shop or to own a sales, installation, and service shop. However, there are many fine jobs in this field, and it offers a good chance for a beginner to gain practical field experience in a busy shop.

The best time to apply for such jobs is in the off-season when shop owners, or service managers, have time to interview and investigate the qualifications of an applicant. Since this is a seasonal job, and the skill requirements are not high, good sponsorship can be very helpful to a job seeker. Another important element is the fact that a shop owner must line up his rush-season crew well in advance, and good sponsorship gives him some assurance that the man will stay through the season.

Probably the best opportunity for a student-worker who wanted to work for a season in an automotive air-conditioning shop would be to attend a training school sponsored by an equipment manufacturer. The schools are open to the employees of any shop where a substantial amount of equipment is sold, installed, and serviced. The classes and shop demonstrations usually run for from three to five days, and there is no tuition fee. However, many employers are reluctant to send employees to these schools, because they are required to pay wages and travel expenses. An ambitious man might find it expedient to make some concessions.

TRUCK-CAB AIR CONDITIONING

Truck-cab air conditioning is another fast-growing field, and the job opportunities are very similar to those found in automotive air conditioning. Truck-cab air conditioning falls into two classes: Class 1 includes pickup trucks, delivery vans, and light- to medium-weight commercial vehicles; Class 2 includes all heavy-duty trucks. The air-conditioning equipment used on large trucks is quite different from that used on passenger cars and light commercial vehicles, and the service and installation problems are somewhat more complex.

The compressor for a truck air-conditioning unit usually is mounted on the side of the main drive engine and takes its power from a pulley on the fan hub or auxiliary drive. The condensing unit is mounted on the top of the truck cab, with the cooling coil extending into the cab. This means long runs for the suction and discharge hoses and for the electric wiring. In addition, road action of the truck body and vibration from the diesel engine can cause installation and operational problems.

Many truck-cab air-conditioning sales, installation, and service agencies are run in conjunction with a transport refrigeration shop, and the mechanics must be qualified in both classes of work. Transport refrigeration shops are usually located near the off-ramps of main highways or freeways. Some are factory branch shops, but many are owned by independent operators. The approach to a job in this field would be much the same as that used to find a job in automotive air conditioning.

TRUCK TRANSPORT REFRIGERATION

Truck transport refrigeration and truck-cab air conditioning form a highly specialized branch of the industry. In some respects it has the same problems and the same possibilities as automotive air conditioning. However, there is one important

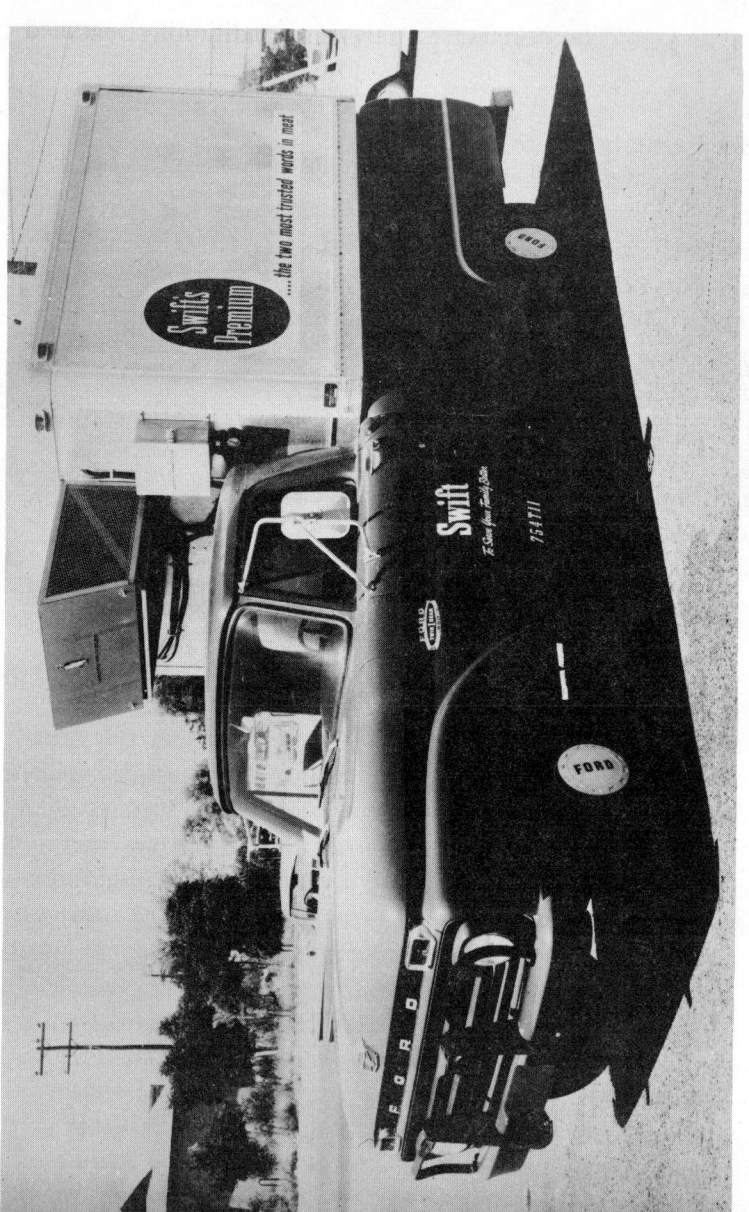

PHOTO BY REFRIGERATED TRANSPORTER

The latest model of Arctic Traveler's Koolvan Series refrigeration is designed for installation on the forward wall of straight trucks. For economical power, the compressor for in-transit operation is mounted on the truck engine.

AUTOMOTIVE AIR CONDITIONING

difference—truck transport refrigeration is much less subject to seasonal swings. The decision to have air conditioning installed in a private automobile or commercial vehicle is made at the discretion of the owner, but transport refrigeration equipment is installed and maintained as a matter of necessity.

Automotive and Class 1 truck air conditioning requires only limited skill and experience, but the mechanics who install, service, and maintain transport refrigeration equipment must have training and experience equivalent to the journeyman level. A large refrigerated truck and trailer unit may represent an investment of $60,000 or more, and the value of the cargo could double this figure. Truck owners are reluctant to entrust the care of such equipment to half-trained mechanics.

Men who hope to gain experience in this field are fortunate in the fact that many transport refrigeration shops also do Class 1 and Class 2 truck-cab air conditioning. The busy season for these specialties coincides with the busiest season for transport refrigeration, and many shops hire extra men for the summer months. The hiring procedure is much the same as for automotive air conditioning, but jobs in this field are not limited to shops that accommodate freeway traffic. Many good jobs are to be found with meat-packing and -distributing companies; food processors and distributors; dairy companies and creameries; and with the big fleet operators such as railroad, truck, and shipping lines.

The manufacturers of automotive and truck-cab air conditioning and transport refrigeration equipment operate many schools to train men for this field. A course of training might run from three weeks to six months. For information, write to any of the manufacturers of this equipment, or apply at local shops. Following is a partial list of the most active training sources:

Frigiking Co., Division of Cummins Engine Co., 10858 Harry Hines Boulevard, Dallas, Texas 75220.

Thermo-King Corp., 314 West 90th Street, Minneapolis, Minnesota 55420.

A.R.A. Company, P.O. Box 870, Grand Prairie, Texas, 75050
Carrier-Transicold, Carrier Parkway, Syracuse, New York 13201.
John E. Mitchell Company, 3800 Commerce Street, Dallas, Texas 75226.
Kysor Industrial Corporation, East Blackhawk Drive, Byron, Illinois 61010.

A comprehensive textbook on the subject of auto air-conditioning installation and service procedures is *Automotive Air Conditioning* by Boyce H. Dwiggins. For information write to Delmar Publishers Incorporated, Mountainview Avenue, Albany, New York 12205.

NONMECHANICAL REFRIGERATION

There are several nonmechanical methods for refrigerating cargo being transported by air, rail, truck, or ship, and every mechanic who works in any branch of transport refrigeration should have some knowledge of them. Many old-line refrigeration installation and service men have a tendency to avoid or ignore all nonmechanical methods, but with the development of new techniques for the use of liquid nitrogen in the transportation of perishable products, this attitude is most unwise.

The four principal forms of nonmechanical refrigeration are: (1) liquid nitrogen for both long-haul and local delivery; (2) liquid nitrogen for food processing; (3) holdover plate type evaporators and a central refrigeration plant; and (4) nonmechanical refrigeration by means of dry ice bunkers and blowers.

For information on liquid nitrogen transport refrigeration write to:
Union Carbide Corporation, Linde Division, 270 Park Avenue, New York, New York 10017.

PHOTO BY JOHN E. MITCHELL COMPANY

A variation of automotive air conditioning is shown with twin truck-cab air conditioners mounted on the roof of a small bus. This type of equipment can also be used on plant nursery delivery trucks where low temperatures are not required. Mark IV equipment.

PHOTO BY TRANSICOLD

A newly designed truck-cab air conditioner by Transicold gives much better air distribution in the cab; the duct can be extended into the sleeper.

National Cylinder Gas Division of Chemetron Corporation, 840 North Michigan Avenue, Chicago, Illinois 60611.

For information on holdover type evaporators for transport refrigeration write to:
Dole Refrigeration Co., 5910 North Pulaski Road, Chicago, Illinois, 60646.
Thermo Equipment Corporation, 179 Pulaski Street, Newark, New Jersey 07105.
Tranter Mfg., Inc., 735 East Hazel Street, Lansing, Michigan 48909.

For information on dry ice bunkers write to:
Foster-Built Bunkers, Inc., 259 North California Avenue, Chicago, Illinois 60612.

CHAPTER VIII

Sales Jobs

Every technician and mechanic who is employed by a sales, installation, and service contractor is expected to push the sale of parts, supplies, fixtures, equipment, and contract service. This method of boosting sales is as old as the refrigeration and air-conditioning industry, and employers have always been willing to offer some form of incentive pay for such effort.

This approach to sales of replacement equipment and fixtures has always been successful because the technician or mechanic is in direct communication with the customer and is in a position to know when each customer should be in the market for new fixtures or may need to expand an existing plant. The intent of incentive pay for this purpose is to stimulate the field service men to take a greater interest in sales. In most instances, incentive is not paid for sales that stem from a major breakdown or normal overhaul of equipment, unless, of course, the technician or mechanic is directly involved in bringing the work to the shop.

FULL-TIME SELLING JOBS

Most sales managers agree that the salesman who knows his product, its function and operation, who has the technical knowledge to demonstrate the product, and has had substantial experience with the people who will buy, install, and service the product, has a great advantage over any salesman who lacks such knowledge and experience. This explains why manufacturers, distributors, and wholesalers in the refrigeration and

SALES JOBS

air-conditioning industry often look for men with extensive experience as mechanics and technicians when they need a salesman. It also explains why so many successful salesmen and sales engineers formerly held jobs as technicians, mechanics, estimators, and specialists in refrigeration and air-conditioning installation, operation, maintenance, and service.

It would not be possible to estimate the number of salesmen who are employed full time, directly and indirectly, in the sale of parts, supplies, chemicals, refrigerants, components, and equipment for heating, air conditioning, refrigerating, and related fields, but the number is large. The 1977 Directory for the Refrigeration and Air Conditioning Industry (published each year by *Air Conditioning, Heating and Refrigeration News*) gave the following listings:

Product Listings	12,500
Trade-Name Listings	2,800
Equipment Manufacturers	900
Exporters	30
Industry Associations	64
Total Products Listed (approximate)	40,000

The headings are not all-inclusive, and the figures are on the conservative side, but one fact can be stated definitely—every one of these manufacturers, distributors, and wholesalers must have salesmen on the road. Prospects include all local supply stores, national distributors, regional distributors, supply wholesalers, dealer-contractors, independent service contractors, and the general consumer. In this field there are far **MORE JOBS LOOKING FOR MEN THAN THERE ARE MEN LOOKING FOR JOBS.**

SUPPLY-STORE COUNTERMEN AND OUTSIDE SALESMEN

Reliable statistics are not available on the number of men employed as countermen and outside salesmen by local and regional independent supply stores, but again, it is large. And to it must be added the men employed by dealer-contractors, the plant engineers who must stock a quantity of spare parts and suppliers, the independent service contractors who must carry a stock of parts and supplies on service trucks, and the supply stores that stock refrigeration and air-conditioning supplies and equipment. Each of these agencies must have an employee who devotes time and effort to estimating future needs and ordering, receiving, and storing these items. In fact, this activity is so important that careless or inefficient handling of it can lead to financial disaster.

Probably the largest single employer of clerks, countermen, and outside salesmen are the owners of the 1,500 independent refrigeration and air-conditioning supply stores that are located in every state and in several foreign countries. (This does not include the vast distribution network of major manufacturers in the industry.)

Sales jobs in local supply stores fall into two categories. The first group includes clerks and countermen who serve the dealer-contractors, mechanics, technicians, and operation engineers who buy supplies and parts in these stores. Many of these salesmen formerly worked as service and installation mechanics or technicians and are acquainted with most of the customers they serve. The qualifications for these jobs include a sound knowledge of refrigeration and air-conditioning technology, parts, supplies, catalogs, and ordering and billing procedures, plus a proven ability to deal with the public.

The second group of local supply-house employees includes all outside salesmen. These men, as their title implies, cover the local territory on a regular schedule and solicit business from builders, dealer-contractors, service contractors, plant engineers, industrial purchasing agents, and other prospects.

The best source of information on job opportunities in this field would be the owners, managers, and personnel of these stores. Further information can be obtained from any of the six associations that represent this branch of the industry, which are

PHOTO BY AIR CONDITIONING, HEATING & REFRIGERATION NEWS

Roof-mounted air-conditioning units of the type shown in this photograph are growing in popularity. They are used most widely where winter temperatures are fairly mild, and they work out very well on one-story buildings.

listed in Chapter XIII. Some of these trade associations carry on rather extensive training programs.

Another very good source of information would be the trade journals. All of these industry publications carry some classified and display ads for salesmen, but some have more industry-wide help-wanted ads than others. A recent issue of *Air Conditioning, Heating and Refrigeration News* had twelve help-wanted salesman ads. Some of these employers seek graduate engineers, but most will consider applicants who have a good background in refrigeration and air-conditioning technology, plus field experience in installation, operation, and service.

The refrigeration and air-conditioning supply house plays an important part in the activities of every man who works in any branch of refrigeration and air-conditioning sales, installation, operation, and service, and this subject should be included in every technical training program. For men who are unable to attend formal classes in this subject, the following sources of information are available:

The Harry Alter Company, with eleven national locations, is one of the largest independent distributors of parts, components, tools, and instruments for the refrigeration and air-conditioning industry. Their 344-page catalog (*Dependabook*) is available to qualified sales and service firms and to schools. Under certain conditions it might be possible for an individual to obtain a copy. Write to: Harry Alter Company, Inc., 2399 South Archer Avenue, Chicago, Illinois 60616, or one of the branch stores.

The Howard Refrigerator Company, Inc., Grant Avenue and Blue Grass Road, Philadelphia, Pennsylvania 19114, offers five catalogs free to schools and qualified sales and service agencies, and at a charge of $5 to others.

Other sales and marketing booklets and literature are available free, or at nominal cost, from:

Bendix-Westinghouse, Refrigeration Products Division, 950 East Virginia Street, Evansville, Indiana 47717.

SALES JOBS

Carrier Air Conditioning Co., Carrier Parkway, Syracuse, New York 13201.

Lennox Industries Inc., 200 South 12th Avenue, Marshalltown, Iowa 50158.

The Refrigeration Service Engineers Society, Educational Library, 2720 Des Plaines Avenue, Des Plaines, Illinois 60018. Material on sales and marketing is available free to members.

CHAPTER IX

Your Own Business as a Contractor-Serviceman

When one seeks to present information on a subject that is not well known, it is difficult to choose a method that will establish instant communication. However, in the case of an independent business such as that operated by a contractor-serviceman, it is not at all hard to show why such a business has a very good chance to succeed. All of the needed information is contained in a booklet that was prepared and circulated by the real professionals in this business—the Refrigeration, Air Conditioning and Heating Contractors' Association.

The members of this Association, which covers a three-county area in central California, developed this little book and circulated it among their customers for the purpose of explaining and justifying the high cost of refrigeration, air-conditioning, and heating equipment service and maintenance. These contractors are all licensed, and all of the facts and figures used are a matter of public record.

In a paragraph preceding the facts and figures on service costs the booklet states, "Your service contractor, like every other merchant, must be able to serve you when you need him. His profit depends on the merchandise you buy from him—he cannot stay in business by supplying labor alone. The contractor must maintain a large stock of parts and supplies that represent an investment of thousands of dollars. He must have a fleet of special purpose trucks, special tools and expensive items of equipment. In addition to the wages and fringe benefit cost of his journeyman mechanics and other employees, the contractor must pay license fees, taxes, insurance, telephone costs, postage, printing, advertising and many other expenses. All of which must be included in the service charge to the customer."

The hourly costs for operating a refrigeration and air conditioning business as of June 30, 1977, are as follows:

LABOR COSTS:
Basic wage for journeymen	$11.25
Vacation and holiday pay	.90
Health insurance and pension	2.46
Promotion and training fund	.12
Social security tax	.62
Unemployment insurance tax	.18
Workman's compensation	.50
Tools, safety equipment, etc	.34
Total Labor Costs	$16.37

TRUCK EXPENSES $1.64

OVERHEAD EXPENSES:
Office salaries, taxes, fringe benefits	$5.90
Telephone and radio communications	.17
Postage, office supplies, Etc	.35
Advertising and sales	.38
Rent, utilities, janitor, trash, etc	.30
Insurance	.19
Taxes	.06
Depreciation	.09
Total overhead	$7.44

TOTAL COSTS PER HOUR $25.45

(Note: These charges are for one, of many, rather high cost areas.)

(*Note:* The figure of $25.45 is the actual cost of doing business, *not* the hourly rate to the customer. In most instances the cost figure is marked up by 10 percent or more.)

The above figures need no explanation, but the bare figures do not tell the entire story. Most contractors in this field obtain the largest percentage of total income from the sale of equipment: fixtures, boilers, compressor package units, appliances, parts, and supplies. When they sell a new heating, refrigeration, or air-conditioning installation, the labor required to install the job is charged at the $25.45 hourly rate. The labor charge for service while the unit is under a guarantee is figured on the same rate. The figure of $5.90 per hour for office salaries probably includes a salary for the owner-manager. The figure of $0.30 for rent and utilities is not high, but many contractors in this field own their property, which would increase income. There is a strong possibility that the cost figure of $25.45 per hour includes some overhead expense that should not be charged to the service department.

The above figures are not intended as an indictment of refrigeration, air-conditioning, and heating contractors, nor to prove that their charge for service work is too high. On the contrary, most contractors are honest, efficient, capable, and dedicated to the proposition that they will sell only quality merchandise and that they will service what they sell. This is a very competitive business, and only the strong survive.

One other sidelight brought out by this little booklet is of the utmost importance to any man who hopes to establish a contractor-serviceman business. If the reader were able to attend meetings of this association he would find that, in almost every meeting, at least one contractor would take the floor to complain about an employee who had resigned and started a contractor-serviceman shop in his territory. The contractor would go on to charge the former employee with stealing his customers, and he would ask the Association to take some restraining action.

The only response to this complaint would be an exchange of knowing looks and a tap of the gavel when the chairman felt the member's time had elapsed. The employee's action is standard procedure, and every Association member present, including the one making the complaint, would be aware of two facts: (1) the member's real complaint was the loss of a valued member of his service crew; and (2) a large percentage of all the contractors present at the meeting, including the member making the complaint, started in business by giving up a good job and striking out for himself.

All of the information presented in this chapter, up to this point, is a matter of record and easily verified. What follows is of a more general nature, but the intent is to show why an independent contractor-serviceman business has an excellent chance to succeed, and how to take advantage of existing conditions.

It is assumed that any man who starts a contractor-serviceman business in refrigeration and air conditioning has had adequate technical training and experience to qualify for this work. Each man must judge his own competence, but he might ask himself this question—"If I operated a business that employed mechanics of my trade, would I hire myself?"

In a service business, where the chief asset of the owner is his knowledge and experience, it is not necessary to have a shop or showroom in a downtown business district. In fact, many successful contractor-servicemen operate out of a well-equipped truck and use a part of their basement or garage for shop and storage space. If this method of operation is forbidden by local ordinance, it becomes necessary to have a shop in a commercial district, but such facilities need not be elaborate, and it may be possible to share expenses with another business.

Every business of this type must, for obvious reasons, have a listed telephone number and someone available to answer the phone. If the contractor-serviceman operates out of his home, a member of the family can take calls. If the shop is in a commercial district, it is possible to share phone-answering costs with another business during business hours and use a telephone-answering service for night and holiday calls, or to use the telephone-answering service exclusively.

Many methods are available to a contractor-serviceman to obtain customers, and the success of such a business depends, to a large extent, on the attitudes and ingenuity of the owner. One of the first steps is to place an ad in the Yellow Pages of the local Telephone Directory. The ad should be placed in all of the pertinent alphabetical listings, and it might be wise to buy a small display ad, as well.

The contractor-serviceman who starts his own shop needs certain tools and equipment, the most costly item of which is the service truck. The truck need not be new and it need not be fancy, but it should be neat in appearance, reliable, and economical to operate. It should also have storage compartments that can be locked for safekeeping of tools and supplies.

Many beginning contractor-servicemen have acquired most of the necessary tools and equipment while working for others. In any case, it is unwise to invest in a lot of expensive tools that may never be used. The following list includes most of the basic needs—

1. A set of mechanic's hand tools.
2. A reliable leak detector.
3. A test manifold, including gauges and hoses.
4. A good portable vacuum pump.
5. An electric drill motor, with drill bits, hole saws, etc.
6. A complete acetylene welding outfit (small tanks preferred).
7. A reliable test meter for electrical circuits.
8. Cylinders for commonly used refrigerants.
9. A small stock of brass, copper, and steel fittings, copper tubing, etc.
10. Printed forms for service calls, receipts, etc.

The contractor-serviceman has the responsibility for ordering parts, supplies, equipment, and refrigerants, and one of the most

PHOTO BY AIR CONDITIONING, HEATING & REFRIGERATION NEWS

The photo shows twin air-conditioning units used on a Ramada Inn motel.

important elements in the successful operation of his business is the relationship he develops with his refrigeration and air-conditioning supply houses. If these suppliers have local stores, the problem is simplified, but every contractor-serviceman should cultivate the friendship and good will of their supply store owners, managers, and sales personnel.

The local supply store is often a meeting place for the men of the local refrigeration industry and a clearinghouse for much technical information and industry gossip. The importance of such gossip should not be overlooked, as this form of communication has social value and provides many good tips on jobs and new business.

Before we present information on a number of refrigeration and air-conditioning fields that offer opportunity for an independent contractor-serviceman business, the following observations might be in order.

In this day of big business there is a tendency to scoff at the idea of starting in a small way and building a business step by step. Such scoffers should be ignored. This method of founding an independent business has worked well in the past, it is working in the present, and it will work in the future.

A comprehensive outline of three types of service operation is given in the following chapter, but most of the information applies to all branches of refrigeration, air-conditioning, and heating service.

CHAPTER X

Residential Air Conditioning Contract Service

Service and maintenance contracts for refrigeration and air-conditioning equipment have been in use for many years, but in the past most contracts covered the larger commercial and industrial installations. The owners and managers of these costly and complex systems understood the importance of having first call on the skilled mechanics and service facilities of an established contractor.

For many years the dealer-contractor who sold, installed, and serviced residential and small commercial air-conditioning plants considered the follow-up service to be a necessary, but unfortunate, responsibility. In fact, many offered service only for the life of the warranty. This practice made "orphans" of thousands of air-conditioning systems each year and put the owners of such equipment at the mercy of any fly-by-night service contractor who solicited their business.

However, not all dealer-contractors took this view of service work. On the contrary, some of the better contractors used their service organizations to build good will and increase profits. Most of them, however, tried to limit service to their own installations and to avoid the "orphaned" installations and those known to be "dogs."

A very good reason for avoiding "orphaned" equipment is the fact that, over a period of years, the active contractor can build up a huge backlog of his own installations, and he does not need outside work. In fact, it is not unusual for a successful dealer-contractor to have as many as 5,000 service contracts in force. With such a number of active service accounts, the contractor must have a very efficient service organization. He must have a crew of well-qualified technicians and mechanics, and he must have service trucks, equipment, tools, shop, supplies, supervisors, and office force in proportion.

Service and maintenance contracts for refrigeration and airconditioning equipment range in coverage from twice-yearly inspection to a broad insurance policy that covers every item of parts, equipment, and labor. The wide-range policies, however, are more common on the larger commercial and industrial installations, and on out-of-town accounts.

The most common type of service contract, and the one to be sought by every independent contractor-serviceman, covers refrigeration and air-conditioning equipment in homes, apartments, and small commercial establishments. Many contracts cover air conditioning only, but in some installations the heating and cooling systems are combined and must be serviced as a unit. Some contracts cover equipment in bars, restaurants, and food stores where other types of refrigeration units are in use, and an effort should be made to include this equipment in the service contract.

Probably the best service contracts, from the standpoint of both the contractor-serviceman and the customer, are the ones that call for inspection of equipment four times a year. The rate for such contracts varies from place to place, but one widely used method for figuring a base rate is one hour of labor per call. Thus, if the charge rate is $20 per hour, and the contract stipulates four calls a year, the annual charge is $80. (Service contracts should never be written for less than one year.)

The annual charge for contract service includes travel time and mileage to and from the job (except under unusual conditions). The contract covers inspection, adjustment, cleaning of the condenser and unit, oiling, and minor repairs, but it does not cover the cost of filter pads unless so stipulated. In case of a serious breakdown of equipment under contract, when major components or controls have to be replaced, the usual rate for labor is charged, plus the normal markup on parts, components, and supplies.

The dealer-contractor who sells and installs equipment seldom looks for additional service customers during the busy season, and this is the best time for an independent contractor-serviceman to enter the field. There are many ways to acquire service customers, and the new contractor should use all of them. In the first days of his independent operation, however, his best chance is with the "orphans" and the "dogs" and with overflow work from the large dealer-contractors, chain stores, and out-of-town sales agencies.

The qualified independent contractor-serviceman has a lot of things working for him, and not the least of these is the customer who feels that he has been slighted by his usual contractor. Strangely enough, the chief complaint of these disgruntled customers is not about the cost of service. Few customers balk at a reasonable charge, especially if they are convinced that they received good service and good value for their money. The one thing that attracts and holds a customer is the assurance that he will be given prompt attention when he calls for service. Especially in an emergency.

SUBURBAN AND RURAL SERVICE

This chapter is divided into three sections to simplify the presentation of information, but nearly every point covered applies to all three service specialties as well as to service in other branches of the industry. However, the contractor-serviceman in the suburban and rural field is required to work on a wider variety of equipment, and many of his customers may be in the commercial class.

The suburban contractor needs the same type of service truck, equipment, tools, and supplies, but he should add pipe-cutting and pipe-threading equipment for pipe up to two inches in diameter. With these tools he will be able to do small plumbing and pipefitting jobs that are required on many refrigeration and air-conditioning installations. (In a city such work might be subcontracted.)

The fine opportunities for the success of a suburban refrigeration and air-conditioning shop arise by reason of the buying habits of millions of customers. Rural and suburban families tend to buy day-to-day household needs from local stores but travel to the city to purchase major items such as appliances, refrigeration units, air conditioning, and heating equipment. All of this equipment will need service, and this need virtually insures the success of a qualified contractor-serviceman.

This is not to imply that city-based dealer-contractors neglect their rural customers. On the contrary, many such dealers sell quality merchandise and give first-class service, but they face certain built-in problems that make good service very hard to carry out, especially during the rush season.

One of the problems stems from the unwise buying habits of many families. If every customer would seek expert advice before investing in refrigeration and air-conditioning equipment, and buy from well-established contractors, the problem of service would be solved. Dealers of this type know the value of good customer relations and are dedicated to the idea that they must service what they sell. If they fail to carry out this policy, they may lose a valuable franchise.

Many families, both urban and rural, are addicted to bargain hunting, and they often buy refrigeration and air-conditioning equipment from outlets that seek high volume and quick profits and have little interest in quality installation procedures and service. Many volume stores offer a minimum of service while the equipment is under the warranty but abandon all pretense of service when the contract ends.

Some chain stores maintain a fairly efficient service organization, but service is usually on a route schedule and response to an emergency call may be slow. In some instances the more reliable chain stores try to offset this deficiency by subletting certain service jobs, often the more difficult ones, to an independent contractor-serviceman. This arrangement can give a measure of security to a newly established business, but there are risks. The man who takes this route may learn, at the end of his first busy season, that his hard work has accrued to the benefit of the chain store rather than himself.

All of these things can work to the advantage of the new contractor-serviceman, but they can also work against him if he does not understand the underlying factors that can contribute to his success. The following outlines sum up the basic considerations.

1. Cost of Service Work

The single most important element that works to the advantage of the new contractor-serviceman is the fact that he is able to operate and make a good profit on an hourly rate for service that is well below the rate that must be charged by the large dealer-contractors. For example, a medium-sized dealer who employs five full-time mechanics and operates five fully equipped service trucks, also needs shop space, tools, equipment, parts and supplies, supervisory personnel, and office force in proportion. His hourly charge to the customer for service must be high enough to cover overhead and allow for a reasonable profit.

2. Charge Rates for Service

Hourly rates for service on refrigeration, air-conditioning, and heating equipment vary from city to city, but the average ranges from $16 to $24 per hour for work performed during business hours. When such work is done after normal business hours the rate goes up from 50 to 100 percent. The following formula for setting rates is widely used: Take the base rate of pay for a journeyman, add fringe benefits, add 10 percent for lost time, and multiply by two. Thus, if the base rate for journeymen is $8.00 per hour, add $1 for fringe benefits and $1 for lost time, for a total of $10.00 per hour. Multiply by two for a charge rate of $20.00 per hour.

3. Priority for Service Calls

Customer priority for service calls is one of the toughest problems faced by the large dealer-contractor. All reports to the contrary notwithstanding, it is never the intent of any service contractor to slight a customer. However, if a dealer-contractor employs five full-time mechanics and operates five trucks, he must have work to keep those mechanics busy every hour they are on duty. To do this he must have a long list of service customers.

4. Service Territory

Most dealer-contractors assign a mechanic and a truck to a given territory. Usually the territory extends no more than ten miles from the shop; and by working a district at a time and concentrating calls, a mechanic should cover from 12 to 20 calls a day. If he encounters major service problems, however, the number of calls is reduced. To avoid disruption of service schedules many shops assign major service to a separate department.

5. Emergency Service

When a dealer-contractor serves both urban and rural customers, problems can arise when rural customers demand emergency service during the peak season. If the customer is an old and valued one, the dealer must respond as quickly as possible. If the customer lives as far as forty miles from the shop, that means a minimum of two hours' travel time for the round trip. If the mechanic needs two hours to make the repairs, he will be away from his regular territory for four hours. If several rural calls are received in the course of a day or two—and they often are—a mechanic might be put several days behind schedule. When this occurs, and regular customers are without air conditioning in the midst of a hot spell, these customers tend to become unhappy, but they would be even more unhappy if the dealer put his mechanics on overtime and doubled the rates. To complicate this situation, the efficiency of overworked mechanics may drop to a low level. The life of a dealer-contractor is not an easy one, but it can often be profitable.

6. *The Independent Contractor-Serviceman*

The contractor-serviceman, who sells his technical knowledge and experience directly to the customer in the form of labor, has lower overhead costs and should be able to do well on a charge rate well below that of his large competitor. If he bases his charge rate on the formula outlined in Item 2, or if he sets the figure one-third below the competition, depending on rates in his community, he would arrive at an hourly rate of from $10.67 to $16.00 per hour. Rural customers would not be charged extra for mileage, and travel time would be reduced, all of which would put the contractor-serviceman in a good competitive position.

7. *Sales*

The independent contractor-serviceman does not, in the early days of his business, have a chance to sell much new equipment or make many new installations, but he is able to supplement his income with the profit from the sale of parts, belts, supplies, filter pads, refrigerants, etc.

AUTOMOTIVE AIR CONDITIONING

Automotive air conditioning has shown an amazing growth over the past few years, and there is every indication that this expansion will continue. It is estimated that 30,000,000 auto air-conditioning units are currently in service, and this number could grow to 60,000,000 to 80,000,000 over the next decade. About 80 percent of all auto air-conditioning units are installed at the factory; the remaining 20 percent are installed after the car leaves the factory, in what is called the *after-market*.

All of these units will need service from time to time, and this work will be done in local shops and by local mechanics. This fact has already brought a high level of prosperity to quite a number of shops, and more will be needed as the number of units in service increases.

Because the business is seasonal (though it becomes less so each year), it may be advisable to combine auto air conditioning with some other refrigeration and air-conditioning, or automotive, sales and service business. This is the usual practice, and a study of existing shops will show how it can be done.

The operation of an automotive air-conditioning business differs in one important respect from other refrigeration and air-conditioning shops, in that the customer always comes to the shop for service. This reduces transportation costs; it eliminates the need for a fully equipped service truck, but pick-up and delivery service still must be provided.

It is not too difficult to get started in an auto air-conditioning service and installation business. It is often possible to make a deal with a used-car dealer, service station, auto-parts store, or chain store to do their service and installation work. However, such an arrangement does not always work to the advantage of the contractor-serviceman. It is often better for the independent to remain just that—independent.

Ambitious servicemen have used many methods and devices to get started in business. Some have been started on the road to a thriving sales, installation, and service shop when they installed air conditioning in the family car. From that point they went on to install air conditioning in the cars of friends, neighbors, and fellow workers. Service customers can be acquired in the same manner.

When the contractor-serviceman has gained enough experience he can consider the establishment of a full-scale shop. The structure of the permanent business will, in most cases, develop out of preliminary activities; but these preliminary activities do not always lead to the establishment of a sales, installation, and service business in automotive air conditioning. In fact, after a year or two of operation the independent contractor-serviceman might follow any one of the following courses of action:

1. He might establish a permanent automotive air-conditioning sales, installation, and service shop that would be the sales agency for a specific line of equipment, parts, and supplies. In most instances the automotive air-conditioning business would be combined with some other sales and service activity to round out seasonal slack.

2. Experience gained in a limited contractor-serviceman business could lead to a job as foreman or service manager in a large automotive air-conditioning shop.

3. Experience gained in this manner could lead to a job as service manager in the shop of a large truck fleet operator, rental car fleet, or commercial truck and car fleets of all types.

4. Experience could lead to a job as director of training, or instructor, in the shop of a large manufacturer of auto air-conditioning equipment, with one of the large distributors of parts and supplies, or in a public or private trade school.

CHAPTER XI

Maintenance and Operations Foreman

There is another field of opportunity in the refrigeration and air-conditioning industry that offers many fine jobs for qualified men, but the training and experience requirements for such jobs are not well known. The jobs in question are those of the technicians, mechanics, service men, operating engineers, foremen, and building managers who are responsible for the service and operation of mechanical equipment and systems used in modern office buildings, hotels, hospitals, schools, and other commercial and industrial buildings.

The education, technical training, and experience requirements for a number of such jobs have been outlined in earlier chapters, but the following story—which is typical of many middle-range jobs in this field—will cover in some detail the experiences of one man in his job.

Cody M. holds a very good job, and the route he took to it is important to men who seek a career in refrigeration and air conditioning; many of the men who hold responsible jobs in this field have a background of training and experience in refrigeration and air-conditioning sales, installation, operation, and mechanical service. It will be noted, and for obvious reasons, that many of the men who hold good jobs in this field are men of some maturity. But if the word maturity brings to mind a picture of a man of advanced years, forget it. Maturity, as used here, might apply to a man in his late twenties or early thirties.

Cody M. holds the position of Maintenance and Operations Foreman in a new federal building that serves a city of approximately 100,000 population. The building is under the direction of the Public Building Service of the U.S. General Services Administration.

PHOTO BY HONEYWELL

The Honeywell Data Center at Allied Chemical's division headquarters in Morristown, New Jersey, enables one man to run all mechanical equipment scattered throughout the 240,000-square-foot building. Simply by touching pushbuttons, he can check some 500 temperatures, turn on fans and pumps, and operate remote chillers and heaters.

After having held a number of jobs, Cody in 1960 went to work for a refrigeration and air-conditioning contractor, to service and maintain a fleet of trucks and to do general building maintenance. The foreman of the refrigeration and air-conditioning department urged Cody to take up the study of refrigeration theory and practice, and offered to sponsor him for student membership in the Refrigeration Service Engineers Society.

Cody did become a member of the Society and was soon enrolled in the night school and home-study classes it sponsors. He continued the training program until he had completed the three full years of work and had passed the Certificate Examination. With this technical training and related on-the-job experience, Cody had acquired the equivalent of a journeyman level of training.

This period of sustained effort had proven to be a very interesting and rewarding experience for Cody, and he now felt ready to move up to a more demanding position in refrigeration and air-conditioning service and installation. At this point, however, he made the same discovery that many other men in this position have made—he could not advance to a better job with his present employer. There simply were no openings. Cody had two choices—he could look for a job in which he would have an opportunity to use his training and experience to better advantage, or he could go into business for himself.

Cody considered both possibilities, but before he made a decision he took a civil service examination for the job of General Mechanic with the General Services Administration. This examination included many questions on refrigeration and air conditioning, but other mechanical subjects were covered as well. He received a passing grade and was placed on the civil service "lists", but after waiting three months he became discouraged and turned to other alternatives. He was on the verge of buying into a refrigeration and air-conditioning contracting business when he was called by the General Services Administration to come in for an interview.

At the interview Cody was told of openings for refrigeration

MAINTENANCE AND OPERATIONS FOREMAN

and air-conditioning mechanics and was invited to take an examination for that job. Feeling that he had nothing to lose, Cody agreed to take the examination, which was oral and was given on the spot by a three-man committee. Apparently Cody did well, for he was hired at once. His first assignment, which was really a schooling period, was at the G.S.A. headquarters building.

Cody was on this job for two months and was then transferred to a new federal building in a nearby city, where he was assigned to general mechanic's duties. He had worked in this classification for only three weeks when the building foreman retired. Cody was upgraded to the position of Maintenance and Operations Foreman and assumed full responsibility for the building. He has held this position for eighteen months and appears to be right on top of his job.

In an effort to show something of the duties, problems, and experience requirements for a job at this level, Cody offered to answer, to the best of his ability, a number of questions:

Question: What would be the first problem a man in your position would have to face?
Cody: His first problem would be to learn the layout of the building and the mechanical plant. It is necessary to know the location of every office, conference room, storeroom, closet, stairway, and fire escape. For the mechanical systems and equipment, it is essential to know the location of every component, fixed or portable; every electrical switch and service panel; every service shut-off valve, and much, much more.

Question: Would a new man be expected to come in cold and assume that responsibility?
Cody: No, every man is given an opportunity to learn the routine of his job before he assumes responsibility. I had two months at the headquarters building and three weeks in this building under the old foreman before I took over.

Question: Are the mechancial systems in a building of this size extremely complex?

Cody: No, I don't believe they are. We have a 62-horsepower, low-pressure boiler for the heating system and domestic water, and we have a 175-ton refrigerated air-conditioning system. There is a cooling tower on the roof and quite an assortment of pumps for water circulation, etc. We have several self-contained water coolers and domestic refrigerators and other special equipment. However, the boiler, heating system, hot-water system, and air-conditioning plant all have automatic controls and require little attention under normal operating conditions. In addition, all mechanical systems are equipped with the required safety devices.

Question: How many men do you supervise?
Cody: I have three custodial employees, one of whom is a leadingman, and one general mechanic. The custodial employees do the cleaning and general upkeep work, and the general mechanic attends to all mechanical problems. That includes minor electrical troubles, light-bulb changes, plumbing calls, etc. I am also responsible for mechanical service (only) at the main post office. I supervise all mechanical work let out to subcontractors, and I help out with the mechanical service if needed.

Question: Do you and the general mechanic do all of the mechanical repair and service work for this building, the grounds, and the post office?
Cody: No, elevator service is taken care of by an outside service company, and some major overhaul and repair work is let out on bids.

Question: You probably receive a number of calls for mechanical or electrical service each day; how do you classify such calls?
Cody: They are classified as routine, emergency, disaster, and catastrophe—depending on who makes the call. However, many calls for service fall into the nuisance class.

Question: What is a nuisance call?
Cody: There are many. The most common is to plug in a machine when the electrical cord has been pulled by accident.

MAINTENANCE AND OPERATIONS FOREMAN

Many calls for service are made because someone in an office is too hot or too cold. If you have three people in an office, one of them may be freezing, one may be burning up, and the third may think the temperature is just right.

Question: How do you deal with nuisance calls?
Cody: Such calls must be handled with courtesy, firmness, and a dash of psychology. Many tenants are under the impression that the temperature in the building is controlled on an individual room basis. This is a mistake. The building is divided into zones, and the temperature is controlled by zones. There is little we can do to change the temperature in a specific area. Of course, we always carry thermometers to check the room temperature, and we check the thermostat for that zone for malfunction. If the temperature in the room is close to the allowable range, we bustle around and go through a few motions, and then ask the person who made the complaint if that is better. In many instances he or she says it is much better.

Question: When you assumed the responsibility for your job, did you find that your technical education was lacking in any area?
Cody: I did find that my training was deficient in certain areas, but the technical education for a man in this field should never end. To be specific, I found that my experience with mechanical plans and blueprints was rather sketchy. It is often necessary to check some point in the electrical or mechanical plans of the various systems. It is also important to be able to read and understand the rather complex schematic drawings for the pneumatic and electrical control systems.

Question: Well, Cody, you have an interesting job, in a nice new building, and you seem to have life pretty easy. Right?
Cody: Hold it! Hold it! You couldn't be more wrong. You have only heard about one part of my job. The mechanical part of my job and the duties described in the job sheets tell only part of the story. For instance, nothing is said about deal-

ing with the public. We do not have an information desk in the lobby, but my office is just off the lobby and the door is always open. Visitors come in to ask all sorts of questions. In the course of any day I might be asked how to go through bankruptcy; how to join the Navy; how to deal with the Internal Revenue Service, and where is the rest room. This is not to imply that visitors to this building are ignorant or stupid. The problems arise because of the *who*. Many people simply do not know which governmental agency they are to deal with. I direct them to the right agency, and most of them are pleasant and appreciative.

Question: Tell us about your other duties.
Cody: There are twenty-six governmental agencies and twenty-six agency heads, plus approximately two hundred employees in this building. My dealings with most of the employees are few and routine, but my dealings with agency heads are quite another matter.

Many of the agencies have a stable work force, but others have a fluctuating work load that is often tied to seasonal activities. When an agency has an emergency—and in some instances this can temporarily double or triple the number of employees—office and desk space must be allotted. Many of these problems can be resolved on the local level, but others must be referred to district headquarters.

Other problems arise when agency heads must call in field men for conference and briefing. We have a number of conference rooms, but demand always exceeds supply. We try to work out schedules well in advance, and most of the time we manage very well, but it takes cooperative effort on the part of all concerned.

Question: Is there more?
Cody: Yes, that brings us down to the paper work, and, believe me, that is no small part of my job. I have to keep employee records, evaluate employee performance; make regular reports

MAINTENANCE AND OPERATIONS FOREMAN

on every conponent of the mechanical and electrical systems; make reports on water-treatment results; make recommendations for preventive maintenance and repairs; obtain bids for supplies and mechanical repairs. I must also anticipate the need for supplies and spare parts, order supplies, parts, and tools, and arrange for their safe and orderly storage.

Question: Well, it seems that you do have many duties and many problems, but you seem to thrive on it—do you like the job?

Cody: Yes, I do like the job. It is a challenge and there are many problems, but I have a good relationship with the tenants and employees and with the agency heads. I also have the support of my superiors, and many problems are resolved without too much difficulty. There are many rewards.

Question: Would it be fair to ask the pay rate for your job?

Cody: I don't mind telling you; however, the pay scale for a job in this locality should not be used as a guide to rates in other areas. I am paid on an hourly basis, and wages are tied to the cost of living and local pay scales. I started at $3.32 per hour, and now, with the change of rate and regular increases, I receive $9.33 per hour. Plus good fringe benefits.

Question: Does that mean that your pay rate is fixed, and that you can go no higher?

Cody: No, it doesn't mean that at all. I will receive another scheduled rate increase for my position and all cost-of-living raises. However, if I wanted to move up to a higher classification, I would probably have to transfer to a larger building. Of course, if the G.S.A. should add another building here, or build a new post office, I would be eligible to move up—if I could qualify.

Question: Is it true, as some people say, that civil service jobs are often a dead end?

Cody: The answer to that is NO, and the evidence to put down that charge is available right here in the history of this building.

Question: Please explain.

Cody: This building was opened in 1965, and the man who held the job of general mechanic for the first eighteen months had a background that included broad experience in refrigeration and air-conditioning installation and service work. This man was transferred to a district headquarters for schooling and experience in a large complex of buildings. He was recently put in charge of a group of buildings and now holds the job of Building Manager.

Question: Do you feel that this is a good field of opportunity for young men?

Cody: Yes, it has to be an expanding field. Every new office building, hotel, sports arena, shopping center, hospital, or school must have employees to hold jobs equivalent to the one I hold here. There is an expanding need for qualified technicians, mechanics, operating engineers, maintenance foremen, and building managers on every level.

Question: Do you consider it a good occupational field?

Cody: How can you beat it? The building is air conditioned, the tenants are intelligent and responsible people; there is a cafeteria in the building; the pay is good and there are many fringe benefits.

Question: It is obvious that the job of Maintenance and Operations Foreman in a building of this size is complex and involves a high degree of responsibility. Could you offer a few tips for men starting out on a job of this sort?

Cody: It would not be possible to outline all of the potential trouble spots, but every man who hopes to succeed in a job of this sort must have a regular program for inspection and preventive maintenance. This program should cover every phase of building maintenance and mechanical operations. The goal should be to anticipate, and forestall, possible mechanical breakdowns and operational problems.

Question: What are some of the mechanical problems that might occur?

Cody: I would rate mechanical problems in the following order of importance—air conditioning, heating, and plumbing. Tenants will be reasonable about minor plumbing problems, and will go to another part of the building to get a drink of water or use the rest room, but if people are too hot, or too cold, they are very unhappy.

Question: Any other advice?
Cody: Yes, if a building foreman is responsible for overseeing cleaning, he should inspect every part of the building on a regular schedule, but he should vary the pattern of the inspection. If he finds evidence of careless cleaning, he should bring this to the attention of the cleaning leadingman. He should also check into every cleaning complaint made by a tenant and take appropriate action.

Question: How important is personality to a man in your job?
Cody: I believe it to be very important. If a man is a loner, or has trouble getting along with people, he should seek a job where such ability is not required. Of course, that does not mean he is barred from mechanical maintenance jobs in buildings. Many jobs in this field do not require close contact with tenants or the general public.

Question: What personal qualities would be an asset to a man in your position?
Cody: Well, I am not an expert, but I do know this much—a man should be clean and presentable in dress. He should be businesslike, but willing to give much attention to details. He should be pleasant and courteous to tenants, fellow employees, and visitors to the building. All lines of communication between himself and his associates should be kept open, and he should be firm but fair with employees under his supervision.

A visit with Cody M. in late 1977 found him to be happy with his career. His pay has gone from $4.07 per hour, or $8,400 per year, to $9.33 per hour, or $19,400 per year. In less than ten years and with more to come.

CHAPTER XII

Financing Your Technical Education

Many students who have the capability to prepare for a job as a graduate or associate engineer in refrigeration and air conditioning fail to attempt this level of education because of the cost. In the past this may have been a valid reason, but there are now many student loan and financial aid programs that can do much to ease the burden.

When the National Vocational Education Act was passed in 1963, and amended in 1968, vocational training in the United States was greatly expanded. To deal with student financial problems many student loan and financial aid programs were established. There are a number of Guide Books and Educational Directories that give information about these agencies and one of the most comprehensive is *The Official College Entrance Examination Board (CEEB) Guide to Financial Aid for Students and Parents.*

Financial aid is available from federal, state and local agencies. Where there are local vocational schools, the Financial Aid Department may be the best source of information. Where there are no local schools, information can be obtained by mail. (Don't forget the student "grapevine.") At $4.95 the CEEB Guide could be the best investment a student, parent or guardian could make.

One of the best sources of student loans is the Federal Guaranteed Loan Program For Students. Under this program loans are made by a local bank or lending agency at low interest rates, and the loans are guaranteed by the federal government. For full information on this and other student financial aid programs, write to the agency nearest your home or the city where you expect to attend school.

ALABAMA, FLORIDA, KENTUCKY, MISSISSIPPI:
Director of Higher Education, Office of Education, Region IV
50 Seventh Street, N.E., Atlanta, Georgia 30323

ALASKA:
Student Aid Office, State Education Department
Pouch F, AOB, Juneau, Alaska 99801

ARIZONA, CALIFORNIA, HAWAII:
Director of Higher Education, Office of Education, Region IX
50 Fulton Street, San Francisco, California 94102

ARKANSAS:
Student Loan Guarantee Foundation of Arkansas
Suite 515, 1515 West 7th Street, Little Rock, Arkansas 72202

COLORADO, MONTANA, NORTH DAKOTA, SOUTH DAKOTA, UTAH, WYOMING
Director of Higher Education, Office of Education, Region VIII
9017 Federal Office Bldg., 19th & Stout Streets, Denver, Colorado 80202

CONNECTICUT:
Connecticut Student Loan Foundation
251 Asylum Street, Hartford, Connecticut 06103

DELAWARE:
Delaware Higher Education Program, c/o Brandywine College
Post Office Box 7139, Wilmington, Delaware 19803

DISTRICT OF COLUMBIA:
D.C. Student Loan Insurance Program
1329 "E" Street, N.W., Washington, D.C. 20004

FLORIDA:
Florida Insured Loan, Student Financial Aid
Department of Education, Tallahassee, Florida 32304

GEORGIA:
Georgia Higher Education Assistance Corporation
9 La Vista Perimeter Park, 2187 Northlake Parkway
Atlanta, Georgia 30084

IDAHO, WASHINGTON:
Director of Higher Education, Office of Education, Region X
1321 Second Avenue, Seattle, Washington 98101

ILLINOIS:
Illinois Guaranteed Loan Program
102 Wilmot Road, Deerfield, Illinois 60015

INDIANA:
Director of Higher Education, Office of Education, Region V
300 South Wacker Drive, Chicago, Illinois 60606

IOWA, KANSAS, MISSOURI, NEBRASKA:
Director of Higher Education, Office of Education, Region VII
601 East Twelfth Street, Kansas City, Missouri 64106

LOUISIANA (In-State Residents):
Louisiana Higher Education Assistance Commission
P.O. Box 44095, Capitol Station, Baton Rouge, Louisiana 70804

LOUISIANA (Out-of-State Residents):
United Student Aid Fund, Inc.,
200 East 42nd Street, New York, N.Y. 10017

MAINE:
Maine State Department of Education and Cultural Services
Augusta, Maine 04330

MARYLAND:
Maryland Higher Education Loan Corporation
2100 Guilford Avenue, Baltimore, Maryland 21218

MASSACHUSETTS:
Massachusetts Higher Education Assistance Corporation
511 Statler Building, Boston, Massachusetts 02116

MICHIGAN:
Michigan Higher Education Assistance Authority
309 North Washington Avenue, Lansing, Michigan 48902

MINNESOTA:
Minnesota State Student Loan Program
Minnesota Higher Education Coordinating Commission

Suite 901, Capitol Square Building
550 Cedar Street, St. Paul, Minnesota 55101

NEVADA:
State Department of Education
Carson City, Nevada 78901

NEW HAMPSHIRE:
New Hampshire Higher Education Assistance Foundation
3 Capitol Street, Concord, New Hampshire 03301

NEW JERSEY:
New Jersey Higher Education Assistance Authority
1474 Prospect Street, P.O. Box 1417, Trenton, New Jersey 08625

NEW MEXICO, TEXAS:
Director of Higher Education, Office of Education, Region IV
1725 Corrigan Towers, Dallas, Texas 75201

NEW YORK:
New York Higher Education Assistance Corporation
50 Wolf Road, Albany, New York 12205

NORTH CAROLINA:
North Carolina State Education Assistance Authority
P.O. Box 2688, Chapel Hill, North Carolina 27514

College Foundation, Inc.,
1307 Glenwood Avenue, Raleigh, North Carolina 27605

OHIO:
Ohio Student Loan Commission
33 North High Street, Columbus, Ohio 43215

OKLAHOMA:
Oklahoma State Regents for Higher Education
500 Education Building, State Capitol Complex,
Oklahoma City, Oklahoma 73105

OREGON:
State of Oregon Scholarship Commission
1445 Willamette Street, Eugene, Oregon 97401

PENNSYLVANIA:
Pennsylvania Higher Education Assistance Authority
Towne House, 660 Boas Street, Harrisburg, Pennsylvania 17102

PUERTO RICO:
Director of Higher Education, Office of Education, Region II
26 Federal Plaza, New York, New York 10022

RHODE ISLAND:
Rhode Island Higher Education Assistance Corporation
Room 414, 187 Westminster Mall, P.O. Box 579
Providence, Rhode Island 02901

SOUTH CAROLINA:
South Carolina Student Loan Corporation, Dutch Plaza, Suite 233
800 Dutch Square Boulevard, Columbia, South Carolina 29210

TENNESSEE:
Tennessee Student Loan Assistance Corporation
707 Main Street, Nashville, Tennessee 37206

TEXAS:
Hinson Hazelwood College Student Loan Program,
    Coordinating Board
12788 Capitol Street, Austin, Texas 78711

VERMONT:
Vermont Student Assistance Corporation
156 College Street, Burlington, Vermont 05401

VIRGINIA:
Virginia State Educational Assistance Authority
501 East Franklin Street, Suite 311, Professional Building
Richmond, Virginia 23219

WEST VIRGINIA:
Director of Higher Education, Office of Education, Region III
P.O. Box 13716, 3535 Market Street, Philadelphia,
    Pennsylvania 19101

WISCONSIN:
Wisconsin Higher Education Corporation

State Office Building, 115 West Wilson Street, Madison, Wisconsin 53702

NATIONAL:
Department of Health, Education, and Welfare
Office of Education
Washington, D.C. 20202

ORGANIZATIONS

In some instances engineering students are given preferred treatment on financial aid and scholarships. The organizations listed here could have information of value to students who seek careers in air conditioning and refrigeration.

Consulting Engineers Council of the United States
1155 Fifteenth Street, N.W., Washington, D.C. 20005

Engineers' Council for Professional Development
345 East 47th Street, New York, N.Y. 10017

Junior Engineering Technical Society, Inc. (JETS)
345 East 47th Street, New York, N.Y. 10017

CHAPTER XIII

Vocational/Technical Education Is Big Business

Technical education and vocational training for the air conditioning and refrigeration industry is big business, but no one really knows how big. Each year industry manufacturers, distributors, trade associations, technical societies and labor unions spend millions of dollars to produce, publish and distribute a never-ending flood of technical bulletins, instructional books and training manuals.

Much of the cost for the production of this material is borne by industry, but this cost is always passed on to the consumer. Taxpayers also share this burden by means of their investment in trade/technical schools and two-year college training programs.

No single directory lists all of the schools that offer courses in air conditioning and refrigeration technology, building technology, maintenance technology, etc., but the latest edition of *Barron's Guide to Two-Year Colleges, Volume 2* lists several hundred such schools. Many of these schools offer technical training programs ranging up to the Associate in Science Degree in Industry Technology. Other schools offer a wide variety of courses that are below the college level.

Another directory, *Lovejoy's Trade Technical School Guide,* lists more than 300 schools that offer training programs in air conditioning and refrigeration technology, but many of these courses are on the Industrial Arts level, rather than the college level. Schools listed in this directory include vocational high schools, adult high schools, community vocational training centers, etc.

Another group of schools whose function is not well known are found in State Prisons and Correctional Institutions. The number of such schools and the number of students enrolled at any given time is not known, but the figures would be high. These training centers have access to the same high quality text material, equipment, training devices, tools and qualified instructors that are found in public and private vocational/technical schools. Plus one other important factor—students may have plenty of time to complete a comprehensive training program.

Still another group of schools that operate in a sort of informational blackout are found in the several branches of the U. S. Armed Services. It is known that the Army, Navy, Air Force and Coast Guard have schools to train enlisted personnel in air conditioning and refrigeration technology, but the number of students in such schools is never made public. In addition, little is known about the quality and scope of training, but it can be assumed that these schools turn out technicians who are qualified to cope with all air conditioning and refrigeration problems commonly found on Armed Service Facilities.

Public and private schools and training centers that offer courses in air conditioning and refrigeration technology are to be found in all of the fifty states, but such schools are not evenly distributed. Texas has twenty-two; California twenty; North Carolina eighteen; Florida eleven; Alabama ten; Illinois eight and Michigan seven. Other states have from one to five. It should be noted that many schools offering training programs on the Industrial Arts level have not been included. For information consult local school authorities and school directories for each state.

TRADE ASSOCIATIONS AND TRADE-TECHNICAL SOCIETIES

The 1977 edition of *Air Conditioning, Heating and Refrigeration News* annual directory lists more than fifty trade, engineering and technical societies and associations. Nearly all of these organizations make some contribution to the flow of educational material that is produced and distributed each year by the air conditioning and refrigeration industry. For some of these organizations the contribution may be limited to an occasional single-page bulletin. While others turn out a huge volume of training material of every sort.

Some organizations have a limited membership and serve these members from a single headquarters office, but many have branches in cities and towns in every part of the United States. Since space will not allow for presentation of information on all of these organizations, a brief outline for a few of the most active will be given. The purpose will be to illustrate the size and scope of this technical education and training effort.

The Air Conditioning and Refrigeration Institute (ARI)
Manpower Development Committee
1815 North Fort Meyer Drive, Arlington, Virginia 22202

ARI is the principle trade association for air conditioning and refrigeration industry manufacturers. One of their most important functions is the development of skilled manpower for every branch of the industry. ARI does not, however, offer training programs to individual students or trainees.

The job of the Manpower Development Committee is to work closely with public and private schools that offer training in air conditioning and refrigeration technology. The training materials they recommend are made available to schools through the training departments of industry manufacturers. ARI publishes a *Bibliography of Training Aides* (4th edition 1976). This directory lists more than 450 items that are offered by 36 major industry manufacturers. The subject matter ranges from a single-page technical paper to a complete training program for a two-year college level course.

Anyone who examines this catalog will surely be amazed by the quantity of very high quality technical training material that has been made available to educators, counselors, instructors and technicians. There is something of interest for students and trainees in every branch of this huge and fragmented industry. Much of it is available at minimal cost. ARI also offers three publications that could be valuable in any training program:

Bibliography of Training Aides (1976 edition). $3.00 per copy.
Manpower Survey Report 1970/1980. $3.00 per copy.

Two-Year Course Guide, Air Conditioning, Heating, Refrigeration. $5.00 per copy.

Refrigeration Engineers and Technicians Association (RETA) 435 North Michigan Avenue, Room 2112, Chicago, Illinois 60611

RETA was organized in 1910 and offers membership to air conditioning and refrigeration technicians, service and plant engineers in food or beverage processing and storage, hotels, hospitals, office buildings, etc., and to students and trainees.

Five study course workbooks, supplemented by cassette narrations and instructor guides, provide widely used training aids designed specifically for the air conditioning and refrigeration industry. Thousands of these courses have been supplied to RETA local chapters and for in-plant training programs, individual home study, use as textbooks in universities, junior colleges and trade schools. These courses are offered to members and non-members.

Starting with the fundamentals of electrical energy, the first course, Basic Electricity, is a presentation of text and audio-visual material in a programed instruction format—a sequence of small steps arranged in logical learning order.

A short mini-quiz is given after each diagram in the text. The lessons conclude with twenty feedback questions to test the thorough understanding of the ground covered. Review examinations of fifty questions are found at the close of each course.

The instructor guides contain suggestions for conducting study or training groups, or college classes. Answers to all mini-quizes, feedback and review exams are given along with suggested point scoring tables to construct final numerical grades for each course.

A beginner starting a study or training in the air conditioning and refrigeration field should follow the sequence in which the courses are listed below:

Basic Electricity
Control Theory and Fundamentals, Part I
Control Theory and Fundamentals, Part II
Industrial Refrigeration I
Industrial Refrigeration II—Systems

A detailed description of the contents of each course will be supplied on request to RETA.

National Association of Plumbing-Heating-Cooling Contractors (PHCC)
1016-20th Street, N.W., Washington, D.C. 20036
Your Future in the Plumbing-Heating-Cooling Industry

The PHCC Association has no direct involvement in the training of apprentices and journeymen for the air conditioning and refrigeration industry, but it is the principal trade association for more than 70,000 contractors. The PHCC Association has, however, developed an excellent informational pamphlet to spread the word on job and career opportunities in this field. The pamphlet has a question-and-answer format and has been made available to schools, libraries, counseling agencies and individuals. It can be obtained from any local office of the PHCC Association, or from the Director of Training Activities at the above address. Pertinent points made in this pamphlet include—

1. The National Association of Plumbing-Heating-Cooling Contractors would like to help you in planning your career in this industry.
2. In terms of pay, steady work and being happy at a job, the worker with a skill has a big advantage over the worker without a skill. The unskilled worker is easily replaced, has lower earnings and much less prestige.
3. The Plumbing-Heating-Cooling Industry in the United States employs more than 1,500,000 persons.
4. If you are ambitious and apply yourself you will be welcomed into this industry.
5. It will take you five or six years to attain a journeyman's position. This level enables you to take full responsibility as a skilled craftsman.
6. This is an industry that pays high wages and whose existance is necessary to public health and comfort.

7. The Plumbing-Heating-Cooling Industry is composed of many small shops as well as larger ones. Most shops are owned by men and women who came up through the ranks of an apprenticeship.
8. By necessity, the Plumbing-Heating-Cooling Industry has become a part of every home, factory and school. Each year new dimensions are added.

United Association of Journeymen and Apprentices of the Plumbing and Pipefitting Industry of the United States and Canada (U.A.) 901 Massachusetts Avenue, N.W., Washington, D.C. 20001.

The Plumbers and Steamfitters Union (U. A.) is the training agency for many of the Pipe Trades Contractors who are members of PHCC National Association, and many of the employees of these contractors are members of this union. A few educators, counselors and employers object to the mention of labor unions in vocational guidance articles and books, but no directory of training programs or job opportunities for the air conditioning and refrigeration industry would be complete if it failed to include information about the apprentice training programs that are available through the United Association and its Local Union.

In the new construction fields, especially in the larger commercial and industrial areas, it would be safe to say that members of this union install up to eighty percent of all new air conditioning and refrigeration systems that are built each year. It can also be assumed that the PHCC, and their apprentice and journeyman technicians, service most of the equipment they sell and install.

The Plumbers and Steamfitters Union has 325,000 members, including more than 25,000 apprentice members. It is known that the United Association spends more than one million dollars each year on training for apprentices and journeymen. Much of this money is in the form of grants to Local Unions. No one knows how much money is spent each year by the 500 Local Unions, but some knowledgeable individuals place the figure above ten million dollars. For information write to the U. A., or contact the Local Union for your area.

The Refrigeration Service Engineers Society (RSES)
2720 Des Plaines Avenue, Des Plaines, Illinois 60018

Since the Refrigeration Service Engineers Society was established in 1933 as a non-profit educational society for the air conditioning and refrigeration industry it has played an important part in the training and development of skilled technicians for every branch of the industry. The Society has more than 20,000 members and 300 Local Chapters in the United States and Canada.

RSES offers three courses in air conditioning and refrigeration technology, three courses in electrical service and develops new training programs as the need arises. All courses are designed to combine home study and classroom work with on-the-job training. All training programs are progressive, from elementary to advanced technical subjects, and a minimum of three years is required to complete the entire package. This level of technical education should prepare the trainee for the RSES Certificate Member Examination (about equivalent to the journeyman level of training).

Most student members of RSES are employed in some branch of air conditioning and refrigeration, including sales, installation, maintenance, service and operations. The trainees work in close association with highly skilled instructors, technicians and industry employers. In fact, RSES membership includes a high percentage of successful independent shop owners. When properly used by student-trainees, this method of training is without equal.

Since it was established in 1933 RSES has been responsible for the training and development of thousands of skilled technicians. Each year several thousand students enroll in these training programs, but not all complete the entire program. A high percentage of students are first-year beginners, but hundreds of veteran members are engaged in a personal effort to update technical education and job skills to meet the demands of changing industry technology.

CHAPTER XIV

Directory

INDUSTRY TRADE JOURNALS

The latest edition of *Standard Periodical Directory*, lists more than 150 trade magazines for the plumbing, heating, refrigeration and air conditioning industry. Many of these publications, however, are highly specialized and would be of little value to the average student or trainee.

All of the general interest trade journals for the air conditioning and refrigeration industry have a staff of competent editors, reporters and feature writers who make a dedicated effort to provide an interesting mix of news items and trade, business, engineering and technical information to the attention of their readers. None of these publications is directly involved in the training effort, in the sense that they offer courses in air conditioning and refrigeration technology, but most of them publish technical books and information of current interest.

The following list includes magazines of broadest general interest. They publish news items from all over the world, reports on new equipment and technical developments and many letters from readers. The advertisements provide an ever-changing catalog of industry products and services. The classified section for some of these magazines can be very revealing of industry trends.

ASHRAE Journal
345 East 47th Street, New York, N. Y. 10017

Air Conditioning, Heating and Refrigeration News
P. O. Box 6000, Birmingham, Michigan 48012

Contractor
Berkshire Common, Pittsfield, Massachusetts 01201

D/E Journal
522 North State Road, Briarcliff Manor, New York 10510

Snips Magazine
407 Mannheim Road, Bellwood, Illinois 60104

Indoor Comfort News
3055 Overland Avenue, Los Angeles, California 90034

Refrigeration Service and Contracting
2720 Des Plaines Avenue, Des Plaines, Illinois 60018

Plant Engineering
308 East James Street, Barrington, Illinois 60010

Mobile Air Conditioning
6116 North Central Expressway, Dallas, Texas 75206

Heating/Plumbing/Air Conditioning
385 The West Mall-Ste. 267, Etobicoke, Ontario M9C IE7

REFERENCE, TECHNICAL AND TEXTBOOKS

Many air conditioning and refrigeration industry trade associations, trade/technical societies and trade journals publish textbooks, technical books and special publications for this industry. They sell a lot of such material, but the dollar totals for sales is not known. It would be difficult to estimate the value of such books to the average student, trainee or technician. In fact, most of the books produced by these specialty publishers are high in quality, but this could have little meaning. Technical and reference books have their greatest value when they are matched to the needs of the individual.

INDUSTRY CATALOGS AND DIRECTORIES

No directory of training materials for the air conditioning and refrigeration industry would be complete if it failed to mention industry catalogs and directories. These publications are of vital importance to every student, trainee, technicians, supervisor and employer in any branch of this industry. In fact, it would be impossible for any dealer/contractor, service contractor, plant manager or stock room supervisor to operate without them.

If any vocational/technical school or industry sponsored training programs fails to cover this subject, the job-wise trainee or technician will seek out his own sources of information. There is both an art and a science involved in the use of catalogs and directories, and proficiency does not come by accident. It comes from knowing the subject and from practice.

INDUSTRY SPONSORED TECHNICAL TRAINING MATERIALS

Over a long period of time, the development and distribution of educational and training texts for the air conditioning and refrigeration industry has become very big business. So big, in fact, that many industry manufacturers and sales agencies list all training materials in a separate catalog. These catalogs are made available to franchised dealers, dealer/contractors, service contractors, schools, instructors, training program directors, technician employees of industry employers, and other individuals.

It would not be feasible to list all of the industry manufacturers and sales agencies who offer technical materials and training programs, but the corporations included in this directory probably produce and distribute up to eighty percent of such information. They will also provide information on factory-sponsored schools and training seminars.

For information specify your needs in a letter directed to the individuals and agencies listed in the following directory. Most requests come from schools and study groups, but most will respond to an individual who can state his interests clearly.

Director of Training
Addison Products Company
P. O. Box 100, Addison, MI 49220

Director of Training
Airtemp Corporation
1600 Webster Street, Dayton, Ohio 45404

Marketing Services Department
Alco Controls Division-Emerson Electric
Box 12700, St. Louis, MO 63141

Director of Training
Barber-Coleman Company, Controls Division
1300 Rock Street, Rockford, IL 61101

Director of Training
BDP Company, Division of Carrier Corporation
7310 West Morris Street, Indianapolis, IN 46231

Advertising Department
Cambridge Filter Corporation
P. O. Box 1255, Syracuse, N. Y. 13201

Director of Training
Carrier Air Conditioning Company
Carrier Parkway, Syracuse, N. Y. 13201

Director of Training
Copeland Corporation
Sidney, Ohio 45365

Director of Training
Day & Night/Payne Companies, Division of Carrier Corporation
P. O. Box 1234, La Puente, CA 91749

Advertising Department
Dunham-Bush, Inc.,
175 South Street, West Hartford, CT 06110

The duPont Company, "Freon" Products Division
Building N-9400, Wilmington, DE 19898

Advertising Department
Electro-Air Division, Emerson Electric Co.
N. Industrial Park Road, Harrison, AR 72601

Advertising Department
Herrmidifier Company, Inc.,
P. O. Box 1747, Lancaster, PA 17604

Training Director
Honeywell Inc.,
Honeywell Plaza, Minneapolis, MN 55420

Advertising Department
ITT Bell & Gossett, Fluid Handling Division
8200 N. Austin Avenue, Morton Grove, IL 60053

Educational Department
Lennox Industries, Inc., 200 S. 12th Avenue,
Marshalltown, IA 50158

Advertising Department
Mueller Brass Company
1925 Lapeer Avenue, Port Huron, MI 48060

Training Department
Penn Division, Johnson Controls, Inc.,
2221 Camden Court, Oak Brook, IL 60521

Training Department
Ranco/Controls Division
601 W. Fifth Avenue, Columbus, OH 43201

Advertising Department
Rheem Manufacturing Company
5600 Old Greenwood Road, Ft. Smith, AR 72901

Advertising Department
Robinair Manufacturing Corporation
1224 Southeast Avenue, Montpelier, OH 43543

Education Department
Sporlan Valve Company
7525 Sussex Avenue, St. Louis, MO 63143

Training Department
Tappan Air Conditioning
206 Woodford Avenue, Elyria, OH 44035

Training Department
Thermo King Corporation
314 West 90th Street, Minneapolis, MN 55420

Educational Division
Trane Company
3600 Pammel Creek Road, La Crosse, WI 54601

Service Manager
Tyler Division, Clark Equipment Company
1329 Lake Street, Niles, MI 49120

Training Director
Westinghouse Electric Corporation
Central Residential Air Conditioning Division
5005 Interstate Drive N., Norman, OK 73069

Publications Department
Whirlpool Corporation
La Porte, IN 46350

Training Division
White-Rodgers
9797 Reavis Road, St. Louis, MO 63123

Publications Warehouse
York Division, Borg-Warner Corporation
P. O. Box 1592, York, PA 17405

QUESTIONS AND ANSWERS

Q. Does the air conditioning and refrigeration industry generate a high volume of technical and training material each year?
A. Yes, there is a tremendous and continuing outflow of such material.
Q. Should the student/trainee or technician collect such material?
A. No, few students or trainees would have the time, or the know-how, to classify, or the space to store, all of the technical bulletins he receives each year.
Q. Does this mean that student/trainees should ignore such items?
A. No, but they must learn to be selective. Practice will develop an aptitude for knowing what is pertinent.
Q. Why is technical training for the air conditioning and refrigeration industry such big business?
A. Because this huge and diversified industry has many branches, and each branch develops technical and training materials to train its own technicians. Profit from the sale of courses and technical books is also a factor.
Q. Why are so many public and private vocational/technical schools that offer training in air conditioning and refrigeration technology concentrated in a few states?
A. Because climatic conditions, industrial growth, and a chance for profit encouraged the establishment of such schools.
Q. Do public and private trade/technical schools train large numbers of technicians for this industry?
A. Yes, such schools provide training for a great many entry level trainees and technicians.
Q. What is meant by the term *entry level*?
A. This term is applied to students who complete a lengthy course of technical training before seeking employment in the industry. As opposed to students and trainee who combine home study and classroom work with on-the-job training.
Q. Would it be a good idea to complete a long course of technical training in air conditioning and refrigeration technology before seeking a job in industry?

A. This would depend on the type of training. Many students who hope to qualify for an Associate in Science Degree in Industry Technology do just that. Such training, however, works best when such students find vacation jobs in the field, as many do. If this is impossible, an extensive program of field trips and job game plans can be an acceptable substitute.

Q. Where do Trade Associations and Trade/Technical Societies fit into the training effort for the AC&R industry?

A. These agencies offer excellent training programs on both the entry and advanced technician level, but many vocational school students do not know about, or have access to, such programs.

Q. Does the average entry level student really understand job and career opportunities in the AC&R industry?

A. There is much evidence to indicate that entry level students and many advanced students do not fully understand the career potential of this industry.

Q. Could membership in one of the trade/technical societies be of value to students and trainees?

A. Yes, such membership could enhance interest in school work and bring valuable contacts with well-qualified technicians, on every level, who are now employed in the industry.

Q. Should industry trade journals be made a part of every technical training program for the air conditioning and refrigeration industry?

A. Yes, students, trainees and technicians should become acquainted with these publications very early in the training effort.

Q. Why are industry catalogs and directories of such great importance to employees and employers of this industry?

A. Because, properly used, they can be time and money savers.

Q. Should industry textbooks, technical, and reference books be made a part of every technical training program?

A. Yes, but this does not mean that every student and trainee should rush out and buy a lot of expensive books. As the student advances in his technical education, and gains an insight into the needs of his job, he will be able to match technical and reference books to his individual needs.

Q. Could you recommend the best books for this purpose?

CHAPTER XV

Biographical Sketches

When biographical material is used to illustrate the career possibilities of any field, the custom is to seek out men who have achieved notable success in that occupation. The biography of such a man produces much that is interesting and of value, but this form of presentation does have certain faults.

When a person has been engaged in a business or career field long enough to have achieved a measure of success, he usually has reached an age of some maturity.

For this reason, and because refrigeration and air conditioning is a fast-moving industry with many specialized branches, this type of biography will not be used. Instead, we shall outline the careers of men who have come into the field within the past ten years. The intent is to show the possibilities that are open to men who seek careers in refrigeration and air conditioning, and to outline the steps that a number of young men have taken to reach a certain level of success. Since these biographies cover just a few years in the lives of these men, it can be assumed that their present positions do not mark the limit of their potential success. In all probability, these men and many others like them will be the industry leaders of the future.

For obvious reasons, names and addresses, present place of employment, details of education and training, association membership, and other details are not given, but this information is on file.

Biography No. 1
The Mike R. Story
Mike R. had completed one year of junior college when he decided to enlist in the Navy. He served two years, held a Store-

keeper's rating, and received no mechanical training. When discharged he fully intended to go back to college, but this was May and he needed a job.

A friend who worked as a mechanic in a large auto air-conditioning service shop offered to help him get a job in that shop. Mike didn't know anything about the business and was somewhat reluctant, but the friend made an appointment for him with the Service Manager.

"When I went in for the interview," Mike said, "I didn't know what to expect. My past work record was pretty skimpy—I had mowed lawns for neighbors and worked at the County Fair Grounds as a maintenance man for two summers. However, when I told the Service Manager that I had taken math, welding, and auto repair in school he appeared to be satisfied with my qualifications. I guess my friend must have given me a good build-up, for I was told to get my tools and come to work the next morning."

"I was lucky to get a job in that shop," Mike continued, "and to have a chance to work with a friend who could help me learn the business, but the best break came when I was selected to attend a factory-sponsored training program in the fundamentals of auto air conditioning. In most cases, such training is given at the factory, but this was a very active shop, and the manufacturer brought the school to the shop."

The training program included twenty hours of intensive shop demonstrations and classroom work. Each man who passed the final examination received a Certificate of Proficiency and a full set of service manuals for that equipment line. One of these manuals contained a short, but clear, outline of the fundamentals of mechanical refrigeration. "I believe," Mike said, "that this text material on refrigeration and air-conditioning theory was the one thing that got me to thinking about the possibility of a career in this field."

When the busy season for auto air conditioning came to an end in early September Mike was not let out, as were some of the temporary employees, but was assigned to work part time in the new-car preparation department. "This wasn't a bad job," Mike said, "and they didn't cut my pay, but I found it rather dull after the hectic activity in the air-conditioning shop. I decided to look for a job that would allow me to work full time at refrigeration and air conditioning."

Mike made the rounds of the local refrigeration shops, but he soon learned that there were few openings for men with his limited experience, especially at a time of year when the rush was over and many temporary employees had been laid off.

Mike stayed on at the auto air-conditioning shop, and a few weeks later, when he was sent to the refrigeration supply store to pick up parts, the counterman told him of a job he might want to apply for. A local meat-packing company needed a mechanic to service and maintain the transport refrigeration equipment on their fleet of refrigerated trucks and trailers. Mike called the chief engineer at this plant and was told to come out for an interview. The interview went well, and Mike was offered the job on a make-good-or-else basis. He jumped at the chance.

"The chief engineer," Mike said, "had a service manual for every refrigeration unit in operation, and for weeks I spent all of my spare time, both on and off the job, poring over those books. In the first few months I had some anxious moments and the engineer had to help me out of trouble on several occasions, but I eventually mastered most of the service problems I encountered."

Mike stayed on this job for nearly four years, and during much of this time he attended night-school classes in refrigeration and air conditioning and other related subjects. This was a good job, and Mike got along well with his employer and fellow employees, but there was little chance for advancement. Once again, a change of jobs seemed to be in order.

A visit to a refrigeration supply store was again instrumental in that job change. It came about because the store owner also owned and operated a busy commercial and transport refrigeration service shop. This man had several times asked Mike to come to work for him, and this seemed like a good time to make a change. Mike gave his employer adequate notice and helped to break in his replacement.

The new job meant a 20 percent cut in pay for Mike, and for the first few months he worked mostly on transport refrigeration equipment, but he gradually worked into the full line of service operation. By the end of the first year Mike had more than made up the pay cut, and in less than two years he had been advanced to the job of Service Manager at nearly double pay.

The Mike R. story is not an unusual one, but one important fact should be noted. Mike could have been content to stop at any job level he achieved, and he would have been assured of a good livelihood. He could also be content to stop where he is at present. (Want to bet?)

Update Note on Mike R.

On February 21, 1968, after three years of steady employment, Mike quit his job as Service Manager to open his own business. He will specialize in transport refrigeration and has already signed up enough fleet-maintenance contracts on transport refrigeration equipment to insure a moderate success.

1978 Update on Mike R.

Over the past ten years Mike R. has expanded into truck-cab air conditioning to go along with his transport refrigeration business. He now places greater emphasis on the sale of new equipment and is a success by any standard.

Biography No. 2
The Glenn S. Story

Glenn S. became interested in refrigeration and air conditioning as a career possibility when he attended the annual open house at a nearby state college. "I spent two days at the school," Glenn said, "and I had a chance to talk to students and instructors, inspect the laboratory, and visit around the campus. I liked what I saw, and the next fall I enrolled in the refrigeration and air-conditioning engineering course. Now that I am starting my senior year, I am convinced that I made a good choice."

Glenn has held a summer job in refrigeration and air conditioning each year since starting college, and his job record is interesting. "The first year," Glenn said, "I worked in a shop that specializes in automotive air-conditioning sales, installation, and service. I picked up and delivered cars, moved cars from the parking lot to work stalls and back, worked in the stock room, did some ordering and receiving, and wrote service orders. The last few weeks I worked as an installation and service mechanic."

"This was a good job for me," Glenn continued, "though I wasn't sure of that at the time. I had an opportunity to participate in every activity of a busy shop, to learn something about work flow, job assignments, customer relations, etc. This was a busy shop, and every employee had to work. In fact, we worked a lot of overtime to keep up with the service load. I made a pretty good stake that summer, but I was sure glad to get back to school."

The next year Glenn went back to work in the same shop, but was soon offered a job in the service department of a shop that specialized in residential and commercial air conditioning. "I didn't have a chance to go on many service calls by myself," Glenn said, "but I worked with different mechanics and had a chance to observe the technician's approach to the solving of service problems. I also learned something of the pressure these men work under when the weather is hot and customers are frantic. In addition, and possibly of greater importance, I had a chance to inspect and observe the operation of many commercial and residential air-conditioning plants."

For his third, and final, summer vacation, Glenn expected to go back to work in the service department at the same shop, but an unexpected opening came up in the engineering department and he was given a chance at the job. "I was assigned to work as an estimator on residential and small commercial installations," Glenn said, "and this was a fine break for me. It was also a very revealing experience."

An estimator on this class of work proceeds somewhat as follows. When a customer calls to ask for a bid, the estimator talks to him on the telephone, at his home or place of business. Before going to the job site he makes a rough drawing showing the floor plan of the building to be air conditioned.

At the job site he notes such items as room size, ceiling height, wall areas, window and glass areas, doors, exposure, shaded areas, insulation, location of unit, location of thermostats, electrical installation required, and other pertinent information. When all job-site information has been noted, the estimator returns to the shop to complete the estimate and make up a bid.

The complete estimate includes a detail drawing, estimate of load, size and type of condensing unit, material, labor charges, etc. Usually it is necessary to get a bid from a subcontractor for the electrical installation. When the estimate is completed, and all figures have been checked by other staff members, the bid is ready to be submitted to the customer, or his agent.

"I soon found out," said Glenn, "that an estimator in this field must do more than just make up bids—he must also be a salesman. For instance, on one of my first jobs the customer complained that my bid was more than $600 higher than the next lower bidder, which is quite a spread for a job of that size. The customer was indignant and I had to justify my bid."

"You can't argue with a customer," Glenn went on, "but I had to convince him that my price was fair. I was able to do this by having him compare every item in my bid against the equivalent item in the lower bid. It was soon apparent that the low bidder had cut quite a few corners. Fortunately, this customer was more interested in value than price, and he bought the installation at my bid." (This is a common occurrence, and it shows how salesmanship, technical knowledge, and business integrity can be combined to insure success in a highly competitive business.)

When asked about his plans after graduation, Glenn said, "At the moment they are a little indefinite. I lost some time early this year because of sickness, but I hope to make it up by attending summer school. If I can do this I will be able to graduate.

"I haven't decided on a job, but many employers send letters to the school offering positions to graduate students, and a number of recruiters visit the campus each year. The jobs are there. I hope I can make a wise choice."

Glenn S. did make a wise choice and in 1977 was doing very well.

Biography No. 3
The Bob D. Story

Bob D. is estimator and chief engineer for a very successful refrigeration and air-conditioning sales and contracting company. He grew up in this family business, which was established in 1900 and has been in the same location since 1911, although the buildings were completely modernized in 1952.

The business covers the full range of plumbing, heating, sheet metal, refrigeration, and air conditioning, plus equipment and appliance sales. During his high school years Bob worked part time and vacations in this business, and his experience included every job from cleaning up the shop to selling equipment and appliances. He was not attracted to any of the mechanical trades of this field, but he was interested in estimating, engineering, and selling.

At the time of his graduation from high school Bob was not committed to any career, although he had given some thought to accounting and business administration. However, his interest in engineering and selling made him believe these occupations might be too confining. His final choice was refrigeration and air-conditioning engineering, and he enrolled in that course at a nearby state college.

Bob had just started his third year in school when the loss of two veteran engineering-department employees of the family business made it mandatory for him to leave school and take over the estimating and engineering for the refrigeration and air-conditioning department. At the time he thought the arrangement would be temporary, but after five years and a part ownership in the business, he seems to be pretty well settled.

When asked to comment on his interrupted education, Bob had this to say, "I am sure that every man who sets out to earn a college degree has some regrets when he has to abandon that goal, and these qualms may persist for many years. However, in my case, I do not believe that the failure to earn a degree has hurt my career. I had completed more than two years of the engineering work (this is equivalent to the Associate in Science degree), which included math, drafting, lettering, estimating projects, basic science, and other essential subjects."

When asked if the two-year college-level refrigeration and air-conditioning technology courses qualified a man for a good job in refrigeration and air conditioning, Bob said, "If a man expected to go into a job that was equivalent to the position I hold with my company, the two-year course would be enough to qualify him—if he was willing to continue his education after he was in the field. However, if a man hoped to get a job in research and development, design, applications engineering, etc., he should complete the four-year course and earn a degree. A bachelor of science degree will open many doors, but that's about all it will do. The real education starts when the man gets into the field and assumes the responsibility for practical results."

Bob D. has not neglected to continue his education, and he makes a continuous effort to keep up with new developments. In 1967 he attended a three-week factory course in service problems on new equipment; and in 1971 he went back for a six-week course in residential and commercial air conditioning. New developments in the field made it necessary for him to attend another school this year (1977).

"These special training programs are very good," said Bob, "but a man cannot limit his studies of new developments to such classes. I keep up by reading two or three of the fine trade journals for this field, and I am also a member of the American Society of Heating, Refrigeration and Air Conditioning Engineers. This organization publishes the engineering Guide & Data Books that are so widely used in this industry. They also publish a fine monthly magazine."

When asked if he made mistakes when he first assumed the responsibility for estimating, Bob said,

"Yes, I made mistakes, and most of them can be charged to overconfidence and failure to be thorough. An estimator cannot take anything for granted, and this can be demonstrated by an experience I had a couple of years ago. We had installed an air-conditioning system in a small store building and had made a fair profit on the deal. Several months later we were asked to bid on the air conditioning for a branch store that was to be identical with the first installation. I sent in a copy of the same bid, and this turned out to be a grave error. I failed to take into consideration the fact that the equipment used on the first job was a close-out and was no longer available at that price.

"This oversight cost my company several hundred dollars, but the loss wouldn't be so bad if you could just sweep it under the rug and forget it. Unfortunately, this is not possible. Your competitors always find out about such errors, and you take a lot of ribbing. For instance, at a luncheon meeting some character down the table will holler, 'Hey, Bob, have you made any charity contributions lately?' And on, and on, and on!"

In talking to the mechanics, estimators, engineers and employers in the refrigeration and air-conditioning sales, installation, and service branch of this industry, one subject comes up again and again—selling. When Bob D. was asked to comment on the importance of selling, he said, "Every job must be sold, but that does not mean that you have to sell the customer on brand names alone. If you are an established contractor, he will assume that you are a professional and will trust you for the technical details. (This is true when a contractor engineers the job. If the engineering is done by another agent, the contractor bases his bid on the plans and specifications supplied by this agent.) However, you do have to sell the customer on the integrity of your company, the technical know-how of your company, and show proof of your ability to get the job done on time.

"In addition, and possibly more important, you must sell the customer all of the equipment he needs to accomplish his purpose. Customers often have little technical knowledge, and they are often inclined to want to go cheap on equipment and facilities. If you can't sell a customer what he needs to accomplish his purpose—you had better pass up the job."

The final question put to Bob D. was on the subject of job opportunities in the refrigeration and air-conditioning sales, installation, estimating, engineering, and service field. His answer, "There are many fine job opportunities in this field—for qualified men. We hire mechanics for several trades (crafts), and we also hire salesmen, estimators, and engineers. This is, to some extent, a seasonal business, but when we hire a good man we try to keep him on our payroll."

Biography No. 4
The Trent J. Story

It is an unfortunate fact that many young men graduate from high school and go out into the business world without any definite plans for getting a job or for working toward a worthwhile career. Many of them just drift into any sort of job, and if it happens to be one that is suited to their talent and ability, it is more by accident than design.

It is always a pleasure to report the activities of a young man who took an early, and positive, attitude toward his career. Trent J. was such a young man. Long before he graduated from high school he had a pretty good idea of what he wanted to do. In addition, and this may be the most important factor, he took the essential steps to prepare for the job of his choice.

At the end of his second year in high school Trent got a job driving a light truck for a building supply store, delivering supplies to buildings that were being remodeled or under construction. In this work he had a chance to observe the work of many helpers, mechanics, supervisors, and contractors in the building trades.

From the very first Trent was attracted to the work done by

refrigeration and air-conditioning mechanics and contractors, and he visited this section of the construction site whenever he had time to spare. Before the summer was over he had decided that this was the trade he wanted to learn. He lost no time.

His first step was to go to the shops of several of the refrigeration and air-conditioning contractors in his area and ask to be taken on as an apprentice. He learned that he was too young to start an apprenticeship and that he would have to graduate from high school. He was also told that the list of applicants for the apprentice-training program was very long and that his chance of being selected was not good.

This negative information did not discourage Trent, and when he started back to school that fall he had a long talk with his counselor. Between them they planned a course of study for the next two years that included shop math, mechanical drawing, blueprint reading, and shop work. Some of the courses would have to be taken at night school.

Shortly after he graduated from high school, Trent appeared before the Joint Apprenticeship Committee for the refrigeration and air-conditioning trades and asked to make application for entry. The committee members talked to Trent and gave him an application to fill out, but they assured him that there were no openings.

At the next meeting of the Committee, a month later, Trent was first in line with his application filled out and signed by an approved sponsor. He also presented three letters. The first letter, from his school counselor, gave an outline of the work Trent had completed in his effort to prepare for an apprenticeship. The second letter, from the state senator for the district, simply stated that any consideration shown the bearer would be appreciated. However, the third letter was really the clincher. It was on the letterhead of one of the leading refrigeration and air-conditioning contractors in the area, and it informed the Committee that the contractor would put Trent J. to work as an apprentice as soon as his application was approved.

Trent's school grades had always been better than fair, and

he had no trouble with the required State Aptitude Tests. In less than two weeks he was on the job.

Trent took an interest in his work and attended all of the required training classes and one or two that were not required. Near the end of the third year of his apprenticeship he arranged a transfer to another shop where he could gain wider work experience. That year he added a course in supervision to his night-school work.

About the time he started the fifth year of his apprenticeship, Trent started doing a little moonlighting. He had acquired a pickup truck and a few items of equipment, and he had a good kit of hand tools. His moonlighting activities consisted of a few service calls and one or two small installations, but this is against the rules of apprenticeship. Trent was ordered to appear before the Committee to explain his actions.

The Chairman of the Committee explained the rules to Trent and told him why such rules had been put into effect. Rules against moonlighting are necessary because an apprentice does not have the required training and experience; he holds no licenses, carries no insurance, and does not have the resources to protect the customer if something goes wrong or if someone is injured. Trent was ordered to stop such activities or face expulsion from the training program.

However, Trent did not stop moonlighting. He merely shifted the scene of his activities from the city to the county area, where there was less chance that he would be caught. But a few months later he was caught, and this time the Committee members really chewed him out. Trent didn't have much to say in reply, and a few weeks later he quit his job, but he continued to attend all of the training classes.

Shortly thereafter it became known that a new contractor was operating in the county area and that his low bids had won him several small construction jobs. The Contractor's Association investigation revealed that Trent J. was the owner of this new business. A howl of anguish went up from the con-

BIOGRAPHICAL SKETCHES

tractors, and demands were made for action to stop this upstart.

Trent was summoned to appear before the Investigating Committee, and several of the members roasted him soundly. When the time came for Trent to have his say, he informed the Committee that he had established a legitimate business and that he intended to operate that business. He had evidence to show that he had obtained a state contractor's license (limited), that he had taken out city and county licenses, and that he had obtained building permits for all jobs done to date. He had met all requirements for listed telephone, established place of business, insurance, and vehicle registry. He had also arranged for a line of credit at a local bank and at a supply store.

The Committee members were somewhat stunned by this display of business know-how, and they asked Trent to step out while they held a conference. A heated discussion followed, but in the end it was agreed that Trent J. had confronted them with a fact accomplished. There wasn't much they could do about it.

The contractors did not give Trent their blessing, but they took no action, and a few weeks later, when his class graduated to journeyman, he was given his Certificate. Trent completed his apprenticeship in 1964, and he now operates a successful refrigeration and air-conditioning shop. In other words, Trent J. took the same route that many others have taken before him, but he moved a little faster than most.

Update Note on the Career of Trent J.

Late in 1967 Trent J. closed his business and accepted a job with a large refrigeration, heating, and air-conditioning contractor. Trent was not available for comment, but in a conversation with the labor relations director of the company, it was learned that Trent had worked in the main shop for a few weeks, but was now on assignment as a field supervisor and doing very well.

It is not unusual for men in the refrigeration and air-conditioning sales, installation, and service field to go back to work for wages after a few years of operating an independent business. Many men make the change because they find they do not have the drive necessary for self-employment, do not like the paper work, lack capital for expansion, or want to broaden their experience. In other cases men find themselves in the wrong branch of the industry, locked into a restrictive business structure, or trapped in a situation where they have taken on too many problem installations and problem customers.

For most men this does not mean failure or a setback in career opportunities. On the contrary, such a change often sets the stage for a greater success and a more satisfying way of life.

In late 1977 Trent J. was still not available for comment, but he now works for a large industrial piping contractor and most of his assignments are in foreign countries.

The ten year update on the careers of the individuals presented in these case histories brings rather convincing evidence of the fact that good technical education, when combined with good work experience, hard work and constructive career attitudes, does pay off.

DE WYS Photo

PART II

CHAPTER I

Changing Fashions in Vocational/ Technical Education

In recent years educational concepts in the United States have been based on the assumption that every young person should have a chance to complete a college education. The college degree was considered to be a one-way ticket to financial success, social status and career satisfaction.

This theory held up well until recently when some defects in this educational philosophy became apparent. The reasons for failure are not clear, but some fault must be charged to the fact that the labor market cannot always absorb such large numbers of college graduates. Plus the fact that many young men and women have become somewhat disenchanted with career status and the affluent society.

In the early days of this discontent with the educational system demands for change were vague, but it is now obvious that financial success and social status are no longer the most important goals for many young persons.

Many of the goals of education are still rather obscure, but recent changes in economic conditions make it clear that the labor market cannot always provide a good job for every individual who graduates from college. This is especially true for those graduates who have completed four years of college with only the vaguest ideas about career objectives and job market requirements.

When the dissatisfaction with the educational system became apparent educators and counselors began looking for acceptable alternatives. One of the answers they came up with was vocational/

technical education and training, by means of which students would be prepared to enter specific occupational fields.

This could be a sound solution, but if great care is not taken mistakes will be made and career preparation problems could multiply. The idea that every young man and woman should have a chance to complete a college education may have faults, but if educators embrace the idea that they can channel many high school graduates into vocational/technical training programs, large scale career problems will surely develop.

The danger does not lie so much in the concept of vocational education, but in the manner in which such education will be carried out. Possibly, the single most important questions to be asked, and answered, should be—what is an education? Should an educational program be designed to prepare the young person for the labor market, or should education favor the creative, social, political and humanitarian nature of the individual?

Probably the most difficult problem to be solved will be to define, or re-define, educational goals—not an easy task to accomplish. In the past the chief goal for most college students was to earn a degree, often in the general education fields. With this degree the graduate was considered to be educated. Not always prepared to make a living, but educated.

On the other hand, the high school student who completes a five year vocational/technical training program that has been combined with on-the-job training, would not, by many existing standards, be considered to be educated. Even though a journeyman level technician or mechanic might be in demand for jobs that would pay anywhere from $12,000 to $20,000 per year, and more.

This is not the place to present arguments on the subject of status for various methods of career preparation, or for various occupational fields. The factors that have developed people's attitudes on these subjects are deeply rooted and change will not come easy.

What might be important, however, is the fact that it would be possible to combine the best qualities of both general and vocational/technical education. Especially in the early years of schooling. If this concept could become a reality, even to a limited extend, graduating students would no longer be limited to a single occupational field, but would have a broad choice of career objectives.

With any extensive change of emphasis from a general education to a vocational/technical education, most students will require comprehensive career counseling, vocational guidance and job information, if these programs are to succeed. General career counseling should start in junior high school, or earlier. Specific counseling should continue through high school, college, and the vocational/technical training program, and for as long thereafter as it is needed.

The air conditioning and refrigeration industry may appear to be an unlikely vehicle for the presentation of information on the subject of vocational education, but this industry has been a leader in the development of vocational/technical education. In addition, this industry has always gone all out in its efforts to provide good training programs and materials. The education and training problems for this industry are identical with problems found in other industries.

In the chapters that follow a great deal of information on the subject of vocational/technical education for the air conditioning and refrigeration industry will be presented, but no attempt will be made to argue the importance of social status and the quality of education. It will, however, be necessary to make one important point. Since it takes four years to earn a college degree in any general education field, and it takes a minimum of four years to earn a journeyman technicians rating, it could be said that the quantity of education is, roughly, equal.

The essential point to be made in regard to the last paragraph should be: since the basic education and training requirements for both career objectives are equal in quantity, if not in quality, any career goal that calls for a lesser amount of educational effort should be classed as inferior.

For this reason it will be necessary to outline the various levels of vocational/technical education that fall below the journeyman technician level. These inferior levels of career preparation are available in all occupational fields that require vocational/technical training. They are also available in many so-called college level technical training programs.

VOCATIONAL/TECHNICAL JOB LEVELS

As changing patterns for education and career preparation take form in the United States a growing number of educators and students will become aware of the career potential in the vocational/technical sector of the labor market. When this occurs many high school students may come under pressure to change career goals.

Some of this pressure will be well intentioned, and will have the welfare of the student at heart; but much of this pressure may have a selfish motivation—to cut down on competition for jobs that require a college degree.

Because of the nature of this pressure every young person who is giving serious consideration to a vocational/technical education should be aware of the pitfalls he might encounter. (As used here the term vocational/technical education includes all forms of career preparation that combine technical studies with on-the-job work experience.) The college level course that will earn an Associate in Science Degree in air conditioning and refrigeration technology is favored over most other methods, with the possible exception of an apprenticeship.

The quality of career counseling and vocational guidance is improving, but it still leaves much to be desired. Therefore, every student/trainee should take advantage of all available counseling, but he should not stop at that point. Each student should be prepared to conduct his own independent investigation of training requirements and job opportunities for the occupational field of his choice.

As a prerequisite to an understanding of what is required for success in any vocational/technical training program the student should have a clear understanding of two important subjects. a.) What level of vocational/technical career does he expect to prepare for? b.) What are the technical education and on-the-job work experience required for a job on that level. The following guidelines are offered.

Unskilled Jobs
Most jobs on this level are casual, seasonal or temporary. Men work under close supervision and no special skills are required.
FUTURE POTENTIAL . . . POOR.

Semiskilled Jobs
Jobs on this level are open to men who have been able to combine a limited amount of vocational/technical education with an equally limited amount of on-the-job work experience. Employees on this level work under close supervision.
FUTURE POTENTIAL . . . LIMITED.

Specialist Jobs
Jobs on this level are open to men who have completed up to six months of training in a good vocational/technical training program, and have acquired a minimum of six months of work experience in one of the less demanding branches of the air conditioning and refrigeration industry. Work activities might include major appliance service, room air conditioner installation and service, auto and truck cab air conditioning, plant maintenance and building maintenance.
FUTURE POTENTIAL . . . FAIR.

Junior Technician
This is a valid classification for men who have completed up to one year of training in a good vocational/technical training program, and who have accumulated two years of on-the-job experience. This experience might include installation, service and maintenance on residential and commercial air conditioning and refrigeration. Such employees are expected to carry out normal work assignments with a minimum of supervision.
FUTURE POTENTIAL . . . QUITE GOOD.

Journeyman Technician
It usually takes five years to complete a course of training and on-the-job work experience to qualify as a journeyman technician.

On this level men are expected to work with little or no supervision, and they must be prepared to cope with all job problems encountered in sales, installation, maintenance, service and operations. Plus customer and public relations for both field and shop activities. FUTURE POTENTIAL . . . EXCELLENT.

Master Technician
Most of the individuals who have earned the right to be called Master Mechanic or Technician will have completed vocational/technical education equivalent to the Associate in Science Degree, and will have from ten to fifteen years of field experience. This classification would apply to many shop and field supervisors, estimators, salesmen, plant engineers, building engineers, trade school instructors, service contractors, sales agents, etc. FUTURE POTENTIAL . . . UNLIMITED.

One of the greatest problems encountered in every form of vocational/technical education and training is the tendency students have of wanting to stop their learning experience too early. In all too many cases, when a student-trainee finds that he can hold a job in one of the specialized branches of air conditioning and refrigeration, that trainee will drop out of the training program. By this action he often sets up conditions that will cause him to become trapped in a job that is far below his potential.

Because of this tendency toward early termination of vocational/technical training, many experts in the field recommend a course of technical education equivalent to the Associate in Science Degree in Industry Technology.

When vocational/technical education equivalent to the Associate in Science Degree has been combined with a few years of field experience, the individual will discover that a full range of jobs in air conditioning and refrigeration, sales, installation, maintenance, service and operations are open, but this does not mark the limit of his career potential.

Additional career possibilities would include engineering aide, research assistant, air balance expert, applications engineer, plant engineer, mechanical superintendant, building manager and many others. Including the ownership of an independent franchised dealership, dealer/contractor, maintenance contractor, service contractor, etc.

QUESTIONS AND ANSWERS

Q. In what way does a vocational/technical education differ from a general college education?
A. Most vocational/technical training programs can be completed in two years and are designed to prepare a graduate for a specific occupation. Four-year college programs often do not stress specific career goals.
Q. Is a vocational/technical education, when combined with extensive on-the-job training, inferior to a four-year college education?
A. This is a question for the status seekers to answer, but two important points should be noted—it takes four years to earn a degree in a general education school, but it takes a minimum of five years to earn a journeyman's rating. Thus, it could be said that the two methods are equal in quantity, if not in quality. Opinions on this subject should be left up to the individual.
Q. Is there a danger involved in the decision to enter a vocational/technical training program?
A. Yes, and the chief danger lies in the fact that students and trainees do not understand the education and training requirements for the various job levels.
Q. What should be the purpose of a good vocational/technical training program?
A. A good program should combine technical education with on-the-job experience to produce fully qualified servicemen, technicians and mechanics.
Q. Do most vocational/technical training programs produce the desired results?
A. No, many programs fall short of this goal.

Q. Why is this true?
A. A fully effective vocational/technical training program calls for a high degree of self-determination and self-discipline on the part of the student. Many students fail to generate such qualities.
Q. What might happen if a student fails to complete a desirable and acceptable level of training?
A. Such individuals are often trapped in a limited skill job that is far below their potential.
Q. Does this mean that all vocational/technical career goals are not equal?
A. Yes, jobs for technicians range from that of semi-skilled handyman to the highly skilled master technician.
Q. Do educators and guidance counselors really understand the requirements for the various job levels?
A. Counseling is improving, but still leaves much to be desired.
Q. How can the student overcome the counseling deficit?
A. Each student must carry out his own do-it-yourself, vocational guidance projects.
Q. What form should these self-help programs take?
A. The air conditioning and refrigeration industry is divided into many branches. The student should explore career opportunities in several branches.
Q. Is this an easy industry to understand?
A. No. The industry is huge, diversified and fragmented, with a great variety of job and career opportunities.
Q. Why is it so important for the student who is preparing for a job in this industry to understand the various job levels?
A. It is important for two reasons. a.) if the student/trainee sets his goals too low he may become trapped in a low pay, low interest job. b.) if the student does not understand the technical education and training requirements for each job, his career potential will be limited.
Q. What would be considered to be a good level of vocational/technical education for the air conditioning and refrigeration industry?
A. The two-year, college level, technical training program that will earn a student the Associate in Science Degree in Industry

Technology would be an excellent, and highly acceptable, level of technical education.

Q. What happens if a student is unable to complete the two-year college level program in industry technology?

A. Any program of apprentice training (formal or informal), home study and on-the-job training that is equal in quality and quantity would be excellent.

Q. When a vocational/technical school student graduates with the Associate in Science Degree in Air Conditioning and Refrigeration Industry Technology, is he full prepared to hold down a journeyman level technician's job in any branch of this industry?

A. Not quite, but when he has completed a year or two of field experience, he will be in an excellent career position.

CHAPTER II

Investigate Before You Invest

When an advertising agency designs sales literature for a resort or recreational area, writers and artists make use of every promotional trick in the book. The descriptive text is rapturous in its praise of locale, climate and fun facilities, and photographers go all out to showcase beautiful people and swingers.

Outdoor scenes are without flaw and the intent is to present a picture so attractive that vacation planners will be unable to resist. The overall picture may bear little resemblence to reality, but this is not important. The real intent of all promotional literature for resorts and vacation areas has always been to encourage the quality of self-delusion that is common to all vacation planners who hope to do better than last year.

Many of the vocational/technical schools and training agencies that offer courses in air conditioning and refrigeration technology, and related subjects, use travel brochure literature to attract students. School catalogs and promotional material combine Madison Avenue type texts with Hollywood type photography to present an appealing picture. The printed text will present a glowing projection for career opportunities in air conditioning and refrigeration, testimonials from successful graduates, and endorsements by prominent individuals.

Photographs will show eager students in well designed classrooms and impressive laboratories hanging on the words of distinguished looking instructors. Much stress will be placed on the beauty and convenience of the campus, opportunites for social and recreational activities, technical library, scholastic standing of the school, lab and shop facilities, credentials of instructors, etc. All of the elements are part of the hard sell promotional pitch.

The sad part of all this is that every word of the text, every photograph used, and every claim made could be based on the literal truth, but still have little meaning for the average prospect who is investigating a vocational/technical training program. Promotional literature does not provide a good base for decision making in the selection of a school or training agency.

When the time comes for a prospect to make a final decision on the choice of a vocational/technical school, the average student would be well advised to pay little attention to promotional literature. When the choice has been narrowed down to two or three schools, with nearby schools given preference, and before a final decision is made, every student would be wise to do a little personal self-analysis in an effort to understand his attitudes toward vocational/technical education. Such soul-searching is made necessary by the fact that most students have been well indoctrinated into the art of self-deceptions about all things that have to do with education.

In the United States all educational activity, from kindergarden through high school, moves at a rather leisurely pace. School activities take only a few hours each week, all holidays are observed, and vacations cut the school year to less than thirty-six weeks. By the time a student graduates from high school he has become accustomed to this easy pace.

When a student does make a decision in favor of vocational/technical education, he must be fully prepared to take advantage of all the school has to offer. Which means that he must forsake the easy pace of early education and adapt his attitudes to the more demanding pace that will prevail in the business world that he will enter after graduation.

There are many fine vocational/technical schools in the United States and a well ordered investigation should reveal important facts about such things as costs, instructor staff, lab and shop facilities, convenience of location, status of graduates, etc. Possibly, one of the most important items to be investigated would be the school entry requirements. If a college level vocational/technical school will accept any student, without regard for past educational records, the student should be on guard. Low entry requirements often mean low graduation standards. Which would not put the graduate in a good competitive position when he enters the job field.

Every investigation should include, if at all possible, two or more visits to the school for a close look at location, lab and shop facilities, teaching methods, size of classes, attitudes of instructors and students, drop-out rate for students, etc. Plus interviews with graduate students, school counselors, employers who have hired school graduates, local bankers, Better Business Bureau, etc.

When a decision has been made the student should engage in a little additional self-analysis in an effort to define his attitude toward vocational/technical education to his own satisfaction. Any student who goes into a two-year college level training program in AC&R Technology with the idea that he will confine his efforts to the thirty-hour-per week, thirty-six weeks per official school year had better take another look at his hole card, if he is serious about a career in the AC&R Industry.

Students in elementary and high schools are only required to assimilate lesson material to a point where they can satisfy school grade standards. The vocational/technical school student, however, is required to assimilate technical subject matter to a point where he can relate industry technology to problems he will encounter when he goes into the field on his first job. This difference is of vital importance, but a great many students never really grasp the significance of this difference.

It is desirable for every vocational/technical school student to bring a high degree of interest and dedication to bear in his educational effort, but this does not mean that the two-year school program should be all work and no play. On the contrary, every student would be wise to have a well rounded social and recreational program. All elements of the recreational program are important, but none could be more important than the bull session.

In regard to the bull session, however, one important point should be made clear—if a student in a vocational/technical training program fails to reach a point in his studies where he loves to discourse on the technical subjects he is taking, that student should consider the possibility that he is preparing for the wrong occupational field.

In some instances lack of interest may be due to the fact that the student has been unable to escape the leisurely pace of early education. In other cases lack of interest could be charged to the fact that a student has no aptitude for technical study. In any event, a review is in order, but no hasty decisions should be made. Awakened interest may lie in the next assignment, lecture, lab demonstration, shop project or bull session.

All vocational/technical school students should be encouraged to discuss technical subjects in bull sessions, but it might be wise to limit such discussions to ideas that will have some practical job application. It is known that many students have a tendency to dwell on the most obscure technical problems suggested by the school program. They love to use high-sounding scientific terms and discourse at length on theoretical ideas.

There is no real harm in such efforts, but if carried to extremes it could indicate a tendency to cop out. In fact, if such attitudes are continued after graduation they may cause employers to believe that a college trained technician is a man "who knows everything, but can't do anything." A ghastly charge, but one with an element of truth. Especially for those students who have limited vocational/technical education to the subjects taught in the classroom.

CORRESPONDENCE SCHOOLS AND HOME STUDY COURSES

The correspondence school and home study method of training technicians for the AC&R Industry has a long and honorable record of accomplishment, but it should be noted that such schools use the same hard sell promotional methods to attract students.

When a prospect writes to one of these schools for information he will receive a handsome promotional brochure—often by return mail. This booklet will have the same cleverly written text material, attractive art work and endorsements by educators, graduates, employers, and other individuals whose names might have some publicity value.

For most schools all claims are legitimate and all statements made in the catalogs can be taken at face value. There will be no deliberate intent to deceive, in most instances, but prospects should be on guard against being mislead by their own wishful thinking. Home study schools often do not find it expedient to point out the fact that this method of training for technicians has certain obvious drawbacks— by comparison with a residency school. They make no mention of the fact that many students do not have the temperament or the quality of being able to administer the self-discipline that is so important in all forms of home study.

Home study programs have always offered a valid method for the training, and development, of technicians for the AC&R Industry, but this form of technical training works best when the student-trainee is working at a job in this industry. Under such conditions the student has the opportunity to put his progressive technical knowledge to practical use. Where it is not possible for a student to work on an industry job during the study period, group discussions and field trips can be an acceptable substitute.

It should also be noted that students who enroll in a home study program are not equal. If a young man has just graduated from high school and has had little or no on-the-job work experience of any sort, his educational task will be more difficult. Unless, of course, he can find an industry employer who will give him a chance after he has completed some portion of his technical training program. This is a very common situation when family members, friends or industry employers are willing to sponsor a student-trainee.

On the other hand, a man who has never worked in the AC&R Industry, but who has had two or three years of on-the-job experience in jobs that call for related skills—such as pipefitter, welder, electrician, machinist, farm equipment mechanic, plant maintenance mechanic, etc.—will have a much more convincing work record to present to employers after he graduates for a vocational-technical school or training program.

While home study technical training programs do contain much of the same material that is found in residency schools, a few important elements are often missing. The missing elements could include mechanical drawing, lettering, blueprint reading, reading and interpretation of mechanical and engineering specifications, estimating, laboratory demonstrations, shop work, group discussions, etc.

Every technical training program for the AC&R Industry, whether taken in a residency schools or home study program, will require the student to apply a measure of self-discipline. Self-discipline is often difficult to maintain, even in a residency school where students must comply with rigid school schedules. For the lone student in a difficult home study program self-discipline problems are multiplied. The home study student does not have the support that comes from personal contact with instructors, fellow students, bull sessions, group discussions, etc.

Possibly, one of the worst applications of home study program in AC&R technology occurs when a student completes a long period of technical study without ever coming in contact with the equipment, components and field applications that he will be required to deal with on his first jobs.

In some instances a home study course is topped-off by means of a one week of lab and shop work at school headquarters. In theory this method works out well, but such programs are of doubtful value for students who have had little or no opportunity to work with the tools, test equipment and other devices used in the day-to-day work activities of a qualified technician.

The end of any program of technical training in AC&R technology always brings a "moment of truth," and the fact is that a trade-technical school graduate is often not immediately able to make use of his extensive technical education. This does not mean that the training program has failed. It could mean, however, that the student who has completed an extensive technical training program, with little on-the-job work experience, will not be in a good competitive position with men who have combined technical education with a full-time job in industry.

It might also mean that such graduates should be prepared to accept jobs on the semi-skilled or trainee level until they have gained the needed field experience. For many vocational/technical school graduates, if they have done well in their training program, any set-back in career progress will be of a temporary nature.

QUESTIONS AND ANSWERS

Q. Do many vocational/technical schools use the hard sell to attract students?
A. Yes, the intent of all promotional material is to present an attractive picture.
Q. What form does this hard sell promotion take?
A. The most common form is the travel brochure type sales booklet.
Q. Is there a deliberate attempt to decieve prospects who inquire?
A. No, most schools are reputable, but every effort is made to encourage self-deception on the part of the prospect.
Q. How could a prospect be induced to deceive himself?
A. The element of self-deception is always present where a promotional pitch coincides with the prospects wishful thinking.
Q. How could a prospect avoid self-deception in the selection of a vocational/technical school or training program?
A. By means of a three-part investigation: a.) The prospect should make a careful survey of the occupational field he hopes to enter. b.) He should investigate several schools. c.) He should investigate his own attitudes toward advanced technical education.
Q. Do most students have rather deeply rooted attitudes toward all forms of education?
A. Yes, many students in advanced technical training programs are influenced by the leisurely pace of early educational efforts.
Q. Would it be a good idea for every vocational/technical school student to get rid of these easy pace attitudes?
A. Yes, the pace for advanced technical education should be patterned after the pace that will prevail in the business world he will enter.
Q. What would be the chief difference between the requirements of early education and the requirements of advanced technical education?
A. In early education the student is required to absorb lesson material to a point where he can meet grade standards. In advanced education the student must absorb lesson material to a

point where he can apply technical education to the satisfaction of an employer who operates in a very competitive business area.
Q. Do home study schools use hard sell promotional methods?
A. Yes, these schools must attract students if they are to stay in business. The prospect may also be visited by a sales representative who will make a personal, and very effective, hard sell pitch.
Q. Do home study schools provide good training in AC&R technology?
A. Yes, such schools have earned an excellent reputation for training technicians for this industry.
Q. How does the home study school compare with the residency school?
A. They compare very well, but some elements will, usually, be missing in a home study program. The missing elements could include personal contact with instructors, moral support from fellow students, lab and shop work, and the discipline of school schedules.
Q. What might be the greatest weakness of a home study program?
A. The greatest weakness could lie in the fact that a student would complete a long course of technical study with no on-the-job experience.
Q. Why would this be dangerous to a student?
A. Because such men would not be in a good competitive position with men who were able to combine technical training with on-the-job experience.
Q. Would a home study student be required to exercise a greater degree of self-discipline?
A. Yes, the success of a home study program hinges on the ability of an individual student to sustain interest and practice self-discipline over an extended period of time.
Q. Do parents and guardians sometimes pressure students into taking vocational/technical training?
A. Yes, in some instances parents and guardians have been known to exert such pressure.
Q. How can a student avoid such pressure?

A. He can't, if he is not self-supporting, but he should have the right to demand that parents and guardians participate in every phase of occupational field, aptitude, and school investigation.

CHAPTER III

Make the Most of Your Vocational Training Program

The student/trainee who elects to prepare for a job in the air conditioning and refrigeration industry, or related fields, by means of home study, combined with on-the-job work experience, will benefit from the fact that his work activities will be carried out under the supervision of experienced and knowledgeable instructors, supervisors and employers. With the added advantage of being able to make use of his technical knowledge as it is assimilated.

In addition, student/trainees who combine home study with a job in industry will bring home a paycheck for each week he works. There are many fine job opportunities that come as a result of vocational/technical education, but success does not come by accident. Competition is keen for the better jobs and all students must be prepared to take full advantage of all the training program has to offer—plus many of his own educational innovations. The same is true for students in a residency school.

It has always been a strange but well known fact that a great many students are able to complete a good level of technical education, often with excellent grades, but without ever formulating a very clear understanding of what will be expected of them when they go into the field on their first job, or jobs.

Because of this, every home study student who opts for a career in the AC&R industry should make an all-out effort to acquire extensive information about all branches of this huge and fragmented industry. Two of the most effective methods for gaining such information, in addition to the material found in the study program, would be by means of the "Field Trip Game Plan," and certain variations of this game that could be called the "Simulated Job Conditions Game Plan."

THE FIELD TRIP GAME PLAN

Trade-technical schools often use field trips to stimulate student interest, but such random trips seldom achieve maximum results. Reasons for failure are: many trips are to showcase plants and tour members never get behind the scenes, the group is too large, two or three students dominate activities, students do not prepare for the trip, tour guides are not technicians, plant engineers and technicians are not prepared to respond to complex questions, etc.

For best results students should arrange their own field trips and the group should be limited to four. This number of participants cuts confusion, but allows latitude for group discussions and review. Trips that provoke special interest could be repeated, by individual students or by the entire group.

When possible, arrangements for field trips should be made in advance. This can usually be done with a telephone call or by letter. For larger installations inquiries should be directed to the public relations department. For smaller plants contact the owner, plant manager or plant engineer. It would be wise to enclose a stamped envelop or postcard for easy reply. Most owners and plant engineers welcome visits from students, but, as is the case with all good housekeepers, they do not like to be taken by surprise.

When a date has been set for a field trip, Game Plan Rules should require an adequate amount of research on the class of installation to be visited—cold storage plant, food processing plant, hospital, high rise office building, sports arena, college campus, etc. Special attention should be given to questions to be asked. Tour guides and plant engineers always respond best to questions that indicate some knowledge of, and interest in, their special problems. Any lack of real interest will soon make itself apparent to plant personnel. In other words, do not insult the intelligence of your host.

The number, and class, of installations to be visited may be

MAKE THE MOST OF YOUR VOCATIONAL TRAINING PROGRAM

limited to some extent by the location of the school, but there will always be a wide choice. The following list is by no means complete.

1. Hospital or Nursing Home.
2. High rise office or apartment building.
3. School or college campus where a number of buildings are served from a central plant.
4. Cold storage or food processing plant.
5. Brewery, winery or bottling plant.
6. Assembly or repair shop for package air conditioning units.
7. Major parts and equipment distributor center.
8. Local supply stores (many trips).
9. New construction sites.
10. Shop facilities of a large AC&R contractor.
11. Sheet metal shop that specializes in air conditioning and ventilation.
12. Repair shop for room a.c. units, water coolers, ice makers, etc.
13. Compressor or motor rebuilding shop.
14. Water treatment sales and service agency.
15. Schools that offer courses in AC&R technology.
16. Editorial office of an industry trade journal.
17. Local meetings of trade-technical societies (when open to the public).
18. Industry trade shows.
19. Transport refrigeration facility and container terminal.
20. Marine refrigeration and air conditioning installations.

FIELD TRIP GAME PLAN RECORDS

Students should not expect to accomplish too much on the first two or three trips, but experience will sharpen the powers of observation. It would be a good idea to carry a notebook for recording data and impressions. When expertise has been developed it might be desirable to prepare a check list (form) that will allow each student to make notes on plant condition, operating methods, preventive maintenance, or the lack of such programs, etc.

The check-off form should include spaces to cover the following items, among others.

A. Compressors, dryers, sight glasses, condensers, oil traps, heat exchangers, etc.
B. Water chillers, water heaters, circulating pumps, cooling towers, evaporative condensers, water treatment equipment, etc.
C. Air handling equipment, ventilation equipment, duct systems, dampers, damper motors, etc.
D. Piping systems, including compressed air, water, fuel, fire control, refrigerants, etc.
E. Electrical panels, distribution system, controls, etc.
F. System pneumatic controls, pressure controls, electrical controls, etc.
G. Special notes on operating methods, operating schedules, etc.
H. Special notes on records kept by operating personnel.
I. Notes of obvious preventive maintenance programs, or the lack of such.
J. Note of location, and condition, of all air washers, air cleaners, filter pads, air inlets, air outlets, make-up air, etc.

The check-off list could be endless, but for best results inspection and notes should be confined to general condition of the plant, rather than to small details. Tour guides will welcome questions of a general nature, but will resent implied criticism. Students should avoid jumping to conclusions about plant operation or plant maintenance. There may be a very good reason for any, or all, apparent defects. Above all, don't be a wise guy. No one likes to deal with a smart aleck—not even another wise guy.

THE SIMULATED JOB CONDITIONS GAME PLAN

The trainee or technician whose first job is with one of the smaller business men in the air conditioning and refrigeration industry may not have to worry about finding his way around the shop or jobsite, but the man whose first job is in a huge plant, multi-building construction site, high rise office building, sports arena, etc., jobsite orientation can become a real problem.

The hiring-in process for a large corporation usually includes a period of indoctrination and orientation. The purpose of this introductory training is to acquaint new employees with plant layout, company rules, safety rules, supervision chain-of-command, company insurance, fringe benefits, paydays, etc.

On the other hand, new hires for a smaller business operation may discover that introduction to plant layout and company policy is much less formal. The theory appears to be—if a man knows enough about a business to come in and ask for a job—he should be smart enough to find his way around the shop or jobsite. True enough, but it often isn't all that easy.

Anyone who has visited a large medical center, museum, or other facility where the flow of pedestrian traffic must be directed, is familiar with the small floor plan maps that are used in the traffic control effort. In some buildings maps are supplemented by colored lines on floors or walls, arrows and signs. Just follow the green line and you can't get lost—it says.

The use of exercises that will duplicate actual job conditions have been tested and proved by Armed Services war games, simulated space flights, engineering mock-ups, etc. Much the same methods can be used by home study students to help them get ready for their first jobs—or for the new job opportunity that advanced technical training will surely bring. Really smart students don't wait for things to happen—they cause them to happen.

The following suggestions for Simulated Job Conditions Game Plans can be carried out as an extension of the Field Trip Game Plan, or as separate operations.

THE PLOT PLAN GAME

One of the most useful devices for mastering plant layout, or jobsite orientation, is the plot plan blueprint. The plot plan is, in effect, a map of the surface area for any building or construction site.

Property line boundaries are shown in their relationship to adjoining property, streets, alleys, curb lines, building lines, etc. Each building on the site is shown and clearly marked with its name or number.

With the aid of a plot plan map it should be possible for any new hire to find his way around a large plant or construction site. The game is to start from any fixed point, such as a construction shack, central plant, control room, maintenance shop, etc., to any specific location, and back to the starting point. If plot plan maps are not available, students and trainees should make up their own.

THE UNDERGROUND PIPING GAME

When students or trainees have mastered the use of the surface plot plan for one or more building or construction sites, the most logical next step would be to a set of plans (blueprints) that show underground piping and utility tunnels. Such plans show all subsurface piping and utility tunnels that connect the central plant with all buildings that are served by that plant. Underground piping plans also show all branch lines, and the location of mechanical equipment rooms for each building.

FIND THE SHUT-OFF VALVE GAME

The Find the Shut-off Valve Game is very essential, and exercises for this game could start from a new hire's first day on the job, and continue until he advances to a job where he can delegate such tasks to subordinates. Every air conditioning, refrigeration, heating, water circulation, and electrical distribution system must have shut-off valves and cut-off switches to facilitate maintenance and service work. These same systems must also have modulating valves, control valves, flow control valves, air control devices, pneumatic controls, electrical controls, and dozens of other items of equipment and components.

When any of these shut-off valves or control devices must be located for the purpose of repair, replacement or adjustment, technicians and operating personnel often have a problem. Either the exact location of the valve is not known, the technician does not have access to the blueprints (plans), or the valve or control shown on the plans may have never been installed.

The possibilities for this game plan are endless, and the fact that it could be a difficult game, does not mean that it should be avoided. Extensive exercises in this area of simulated job conditions will pay big dividends in job know-how.

QUESTIONS AND ANSWERS

Q. Will a well conceived home study program in AC&R technology produce job-ready technicians?
A. Not quite, but a good home study program will produce men who have the potential to become fully qualified technicians.
Q. How much on-the-job experience would be required to produce a well qualified technician?
A. This will vary with the individual, but three years of combined home study and field experience should suffice.
Q. Would it be possible to speed up the internship?
A. Yes, there are many things a student-trainee can do to enhance technical education.
Q. How could this be done?
A. There are many ways to intensify student interest in a technical education and among the most effective are the Field Trip Game and the Simulated Job Conditions Game.
Q. How can field trips be used to good advantage?
A. Field trips bring student-trainees into direct contact with professional level technicians and operating personnel, and give them a chance to observe plant layout, plant operation, plant maintenance, etc.
Q. Should students on field trips ask questions?
A. Yes, and a little advance thought will enable the student to ask questions that are relevant to the plant under review.
Q. Does every class of air conditioning, heating and refrigeration system have certain specific operating and maintenance problems?

A. Yes, and with a well conceived game plan students should be able to spot these problem areas and ask questions about them. Plant engineers will welcome questions, but don't be a wise guy.

Q. Should some field trips be repeated?

A. Yes, several trips to installations of special interest could be productive.

Q. Is it true that employees can get lost on a large construction site, or in a complex of high rise buildings?

A. Yes, employees get lost in the sense that they cannot find their way from a central point to any point on the site, and return by the shortest route.

Q. Is there another facet to this "getting lost" problem?"

A. Yes, technicians and operating personnel get lost in the sense that they are unable to locate shut-off valves, control valves, electrical switches, etc.

Q. How can trainees and home study students prepare to cope with this problem?

A. The best method would be to formulate game plans that will simulate actual job conditions.

Q. What elements should these game plans have?

A. Students must use their imagination to devise effective game plans.

Q. How can students and trainees practice such game plans where they do not have access to building sites, construction sites, plot plans, blueprints, etc.?

A. In most instances it will be possible to use public buildings, school buildings, etc. It may be necessary to make up plot plans, underground piping plans, etc., for a park, golf course, subdivision, etc.

Q. Could the games outlined here be important to a technical training program?

A. Yes, it is of vital importance for students and trainees to be prepared to deal with actual job conditions.

CHAPTER IV

Work Habits, Job Attitudes and Career Hangups

When a student has completed a long program of vocational/technical education and has gained a year or two of on-the-job work experience, he may believe that he now has it made, that industry employers will be bidding for his services. With the ever-expanding demand for qualified technicians in every branch of the air conditioning and refrigeration industry this could be true, but this might be a good time for the emerging technician to take a good look at the employment facts of life, from the employers point of view.

It is certainly true that students who have completed a good level of vocational/technical education and have gained a year or two of work experience are in a very good position careerwise, but the battle is only half won. The technician must still match technical education, job skills and personality to the needs of an employer. It is a sad fact that many technicians never achieve a degree of matching that will lead to career satisfaction and financial success. Much of this failure can be charged to the fact that employees do not understand the problems of industry employers.

Since it is a known fact that this lack of understanding exists, the technician who is serious about his career would be wise to review some of the elements that must be present in every successful business that involves sales, installation, maintenance and service for any branch of the industry. If a dealer/contractor, service contractor or other class of employer expects his business to survive and prosper, he must make a dedicated effort to accomplish the following objectives—

1. He must operate his business at a profit.
2. He must sell new and replacement equipment, parts and supplies.

3. He must sell service contracts and provide fast and efficient service to all customers.
4. He must collect all accounts when due.
5. He must hire only well qualified technicians, field supervisors, shop foremen and office personnel.
6. He must provide technicians with good quality shop equipment, tools, test instruments, service trucks, etc.
7. He must maintain a good relationship with his customers and the general public.
8. He must provide educational and training programs to update job skills and technical knowledge of his employees.
9. He must establish bonus and incentive plans to stimulate employee interest.
10. He must make use of every possible means for advertising and promoting his business.

It has never been easy for employers in the air conditioning and refrigeration industry to hire well qualified shop and field technicians, and no sure fire method for employee evaluation has ever been developed—but not for any lack of effort. Since the earliest days of this industry employers have struggled with the hiring problem, but no lasting solutions have been found. Industry employers encounter the same negative work habits and job habits in technician employees over and over again.

The very large industry employers, who hire many technicians, often delegate the hiring of competent personnel to the personnel department. In recruiting, such departments may make use of the resume, interviews, job testing, employment records, etc., to determine the qualifications of job candidates.

On the other hand, employers who hire only a few technicians must make-do with much less elaborate hiring methods. Since hiring decisions for these smaller shops are made by employers and supervisors who have extensive knowledge of the job to be filled, mistakes are not quite so serious. If a new hire doesn't work out, he can be terminated on short notice.

In their continuing efforts to solve hiring problems industry employers, supervisors and leading technicians hold many meetings

WORK HABITS, JOB ATTITUDES AND CAREER HANGUPS

and attend many conferences. The purpose of these meetings is to develop better methods for evaluating employee potential, and for dealing with problems that exist in the ranks of employees who are already on the payroll.

When an employer finds that certain negative work habits, job attitudes and personality traits occur time after time, and it is known that these attitudes are bad for all concerned, it is obvious that some action must be taken. When an employer has men on his payroll who are well qualified from a technical education standpoint, but are not an asset to his business, that employer has a problem. Either he must fire the man, in the hope that he will be able to hire a better replacement, or he must make an effort to change the attitudes of the employee.

Long experience has convinced many industry employers that it is very difficult to eradicate bad work habits and job attitudes that have become deeply rooted. For this reason, many employers find it expedient to fire the employee and try to find a more cooperative replacement. In many instances employers are willing to accept a technician who has had a less extensive amount of technical education and on-the-job work experience, often in the hope that he will have fewer career hangups.

In some instances technicians can be recruited from the ranks of helpers and trainees who are already on the payroll, or from other occupational fields where an equivalent amount of technical education and field experience is required. Possibilities would include electricians, sheet metal mechanics, machinists, pipefitters, welders, etc. Other sources would include trade-technical school graduates, home study school graduates, and men employed by other industry employers.

Since work habits, job attitudes and personality can be of such great importance to all students, trainees and technicians, it would be wise for such men to give some thought to the dangers that lurk in all forms of negative thinking. With adequate forewarning it would be possible to guard against the unconscious development of destructive career thought patterns, work habits and job attitudes.

The following outlines are brief, and they do not cover every possibility, but they do detail a few of the most commonly encountered career hangups, as noted by knowledgeable employers, supervisors and leading technicians. The outlines have no official standing, but the information comes from individuals who have been out on the firing line dealing with these problems for many years. In other words, the information presented is not theoretical.

There is a large body of evidence to indicate that many bad work habits, job attitudes and career hangups have developed out of a close association between fellow trade-technical students, poorly qualified instructors, disgruntled work-mate technicians, semi-competent supervisors and marginal employers. The information that follows, as it was received from concerned individuals, was expressed in rather strong negative terms. In the hope of achieving easier understanding, the language of the outlines will be positive in nature.

WORK HABITS AND CAREER HANGUPS

Psychology tells us that "habit can be a master, or it can be a slave," and this is certainly true for students, trainees and technicians who expect to work in any branch of air conditioning and refrigeration sales, installation, maintenance and service. The job tasks these skilled technicians are required to perform are so diversified, and so complex, that they could never be reduced to a routine operation.

Because of this diversity, and complexity, the only effective method, and the one used by the most successful technicians, is to develop work patterns that will automatically select the best method for each task. This "automatic" method will work well for technicians who have always used the power of good thought patterns. It will have little or no value for men who have allowed careless work habits and bad job attitudes to take root. We know from elementary psychology that the best way to develop constructive work habits would be to never allow bad work habits to become deeply rooted. Few men can afford such career handicaps.

In early stages of trade-technical school studies and on-the-job training most student-trainees will be given little instruction on the all-important subject of work habits, job attitudes and negative personality traits. These student-trainees would be well advised, however, to make an effort to emulate the work habits and job attitudes of the sharpest students in the class and the best qualified technicians in the shops where they work. These top-grade students, technicians, shop men and supervisors did not come by their good reputation by accident. They earned it by proving, over a period of time, that they can get any job done.

SAFETY

Along with good work habits, and of equal importance to career success, would be the ability of every technician to work safely at all times and under all conditions. When a skilled technician has devoted several years of his life to the acquisition of a good technical education, and more years to gain the needed field experience that will make him valuable to any employer, the only way that technician can cash in on his investment is by working on a good paying job or by operating his own business.

For this reason, it is of vital importance for every student, trainee and technician to understand the hazards of his occupation, and to obey the safety rules that will reduce these hazards to a minimum. Good safety habits have one thing in common with all other habits in that they can be consciously formed. If good safety habits are formulated very early in career development, those good habits will stay with the technician throughout his working life. A careless attitude toward safety, either on or off the job, is stupid. Stupidity always brings its own reward.

KEEPING UP WITH NEW TECHNICAL DEVELOPMENTS

The technology for every branch of the air conditioning and refrigeration is undergoing constant change and any technician who fails to keep up with new developments in his field will find himself running slow in the career race. One of the best ways to keep up with changing technology and new industry developments would be to form the habit of reading one or more of the fine trade-technical journals that are published for this industry.

Other news of interest can be found in current issues of sales, installation, maintenance, service and operating manuals that are published and distributed by industry manufacturers. These publications, along with engineering specifications and technical bulletins, are available from dealer-contractors, service contractors, supply stores, etc.

In many localities technicians will have an opportunity to attend employer sponsored lectures, training programs and training seminars. If at all possible, every student-trainee and technician should attend at least one industry trade show each year. In addition, membership in one of the fine trade-technical or engineering societies could have great value for many men.

THE PUBLIC IMAGE AND CUSTOMER GOODWILL

Because of the rather special nature of the air conditioning and refrigeration industry a good public image is of vital importance. Therefore, every student, trainee and technician should be put on notice of the fact that he has a responsibility in this area.

To provide high quality installation, maintenance and service to his customers, every dealer/contractor and service contractor must make a large investment in shop equipment, tools, service trucks, parts inventory and office facilities. To carry on his business effectively he must maintain a highly qualified staff of sales, estimating, engineering and office personnel.

Unfortunately, many customers are only vaguely aware of the huge investment these shop owners must make for their benefit, but these same customers are always acutely aware of the high charge rates for all installation, maintenance and service labor. They are also well acquainted with the apparent high cost for new equipment, replacement equipment, parts and supplies.

In many instances the field technician and service engineer is the only direct link between the customer and his employer. For this reason, it is of vital importance for every field technician to be aware of his responsibility for being a goodwill ambassador for his employer, and for the industry as a whole. It should also be obvious that any marked ability to create goodwill for an employer will work with equal force when the technician becomes self-employed.

In view of the often critical attitudes that many customers have toward the dealer/contractor and the service contractor, it is important for every technician to conduct himself in a businesslike and dignified manner in all of his dealings with his employer's customers. He must formulate the habit of treating every customer, no matter how unreasonable that customer may appear to be at the moment, with courtesy, consideration and respect.

If any student-trainee or technician fails to grasp these business facts of life, the reputation of his employer and his own reputation will be damaged. To say nothing of the fact that the good image of the air conditioning and refrigeration industry as a whole will suffer.

QUESTIONS AND ANSWERS

Q. Is there a growing demand for well qualified technicians in every branch of air conditioning and refrigeration sales, installation and service?

A. Yes, but take special note of the words *well qualified*.

Q. Just what do these words mean?

A. When a technician advances beyond the trainee stage he will be expected to have acheived a good level of technical education and on-the-job work experience. He must also develop constructive work habits and job attitudes.

Q. When a technician goes into the field on his first jobs, what is the single most important thing that he should know about his employer?

A. He should know that every phase of air conditioning and refrigeration sales, installation, maintenance and service is a competitive business area. To stay in business, and prosper, the employer must be able to show a profit on every phase of his business operation.

Q. Do employers for this industry find it difficult to hire enough fully qualified technicians?

A. Yes, and these problems often have little to do with technical education and on-the-job training.

Q. What is the greatest problem in hiring?

A. Employee problems often originate in the fact that technicians have developed bad work habits, job attitudes and personality traits.

Q. Can the average employer afford to keep these difficult employees on his payroll?

A. No, few employers can afford such handicapped employees.

Q. Will most industry employers make an effort to re-educate technicians who have developed destructive work habits and job attitudes?

A. No, in most instances such technicians will be terminated when it is convenient for the employer.

Q. When technicians are layed off for this cause, will they be informed of the reasons?

A. No. Most employers will avoid a confrontation that could be embarrassing.

Q. How do bad work habits and job attitudes develop?

A. Negative personality traits may date back to childhood. Such tendencies can be made worse by association with horrible examples.

Q. How can students, trainees and technicians avoid the development of negative work habits and job attitudes?

A. By making a conscious effort to detect such trends before they have a chance to take root.

Q. Is a good reputation for technical competence, job know-how and good work habits of importance to the technician?

A. Yes, good work habits and job know-how can pave the way to excellent annual earnings, promotion and career satisfaction.